Probability Distributions

Applied CQRM Book Series

Volume II

Applying Monte Carlo Risk Simulation, Strategic Real Options, Stochastic Forecasting, Portfolio Optimization, Data and Decision Analytics

IIPER Press

IIPER
Press

Johnathan Mun, Ph.D.

California, USA

Risk Simulator

For Jayden, Emma, and Penny.

In a world where risk and uncertainty abound, you are the only constants in my life.

Dedicated in loving memory of my mom.

Delight yourself in the Lord and He will give you the desires of your heart.

Psalm 37:4

The Applied CQRM Book Series showcases how the advanced analytics covered in the Certified in Quantitative Risk Management (CQRM) certification program can be applied in real-life business problems. In Volume II, we show how Risk Simulator can be used to generate various probability distributions as well as how to interpret the results and use their analytical properties for making strategic decisions.

Pragmatic applications are emphasized in order to demystify the many elements inherent in probability analysis. A black box will remain a black box if no one can understand the concepts despite its power and applicability. It is only when the black box methods become transparent, so that researchers can understand, apply, and convince others of their results, value-add, and applicability, that the approaches will receive widespread attention. This transparency is achieved through step-by-step applications of quantitative modeling as well as presenting multiple cases and discussing real-life applications.

This book is targeted at those individuals who have completed the CQRM certification program but can also be used by anyone familiar with basic quantitative research methods—there is something for everyone. It is also applicable for use as a second-year MBA/MS-level or introductory PhD textbook. The examples in the book assume some prior knowledge of the subject matter.

Additional information on the CQRM program can be obtained at:

www.iiper.org

www.realoptionsvaluation.com

www.rovusa.com

Dr. Johnathan C. Mun is the founder, chairman, and CEO of Real Options Valuation, Inc. (ROV), a consulting, training, and software development firm specializing in strategic real options, financial valuation, Monte Carlo risk simulation, stochastic forecasting, optimization, decision analytics, business intelligence, healthcare analytics, enterprise risk management, project risk management, quantitative research methods, and risk analysis located in northern Silicon Valley, California. ROV has partners around the world including Argentina, Beijing, Chicago, China, Colombia, Ghana, Hong Kong, India, Italy, Japan, Malaysia, Mexico City, New York, Nigeria, Peru, Puerto Rico, Russia, Saudi Arabia, Shanghai, Singapore, Slovenia, South Africa, South Korea, Spain, United Kingdom, Venezuela, Zurich, and others. ROV also has a local office in Shanghai.

Dr. Mun is also the chairman of the International Institute of Professional Education and Research (IIPER), an accredited global organization staffed by professors from named universities from around the world that provides the Certified in Quantitative Risk Management (CQRM) and Certified in Risk Management (CRM) designations, among others. He is the creator of many powerful software tools including Risk Simulator, Real Options SLS Super Lattice Solver, Modeling Toolkit, Project Economics Analysis Tool (PEAT), Credit Market Operational Liquidity Risk (CMOL), Employee Stock Options Valuation, ROV BizStats, ROV Modeler Suite (Basel Credit Modeler, Risk Modeler, Optimizer, and Valuator), ROV Compiler, ROV Extractor and Evaluator, ROV Dashboard, ROV Quantitative Data Miner, and other software applications, as well as the risk-analysis training DVD. He holds public seminars on risk analysis and CQRM programs. He has over 21 registered patents and patents pending globally. He has authored over 23 books published by John Wiley & Sons, Elsevier Science, IIPER Press, and ROV Press, including multiple volumes of the Applied CQRM Series (IIPER Press, 2019-2020); *Modeling Risk: Applying Monte Carlo Simulation, Strategic Real Options, Stochastic Forecasting, Portfolio Optimization, Data Analytics, Business Intelligence, and Decision Modeling,* First Edition (Wiley, 2006), Second Edition (Wiley, 2010), and Third Edition

(ROV Press, 2015); *The Banker's Handbook on Credit Risk* (2008); *Advanced Analytical Models: 250 Applications from Basel II Accord to Wall Street and Beyond* (2008); *Real Options Analysis: Tools and Techniques,* First Edition (2003) and Second Edition (2005); *Real Options Analysis Course: Business Cases* (2003); *Applied Risk Analysis: Moving Beyond Uncertainty* (2003); and *Valuing Employee Stock Options* (2004). His books and software are being used at over 350 top universities around the world, including the Bern Institute in Germany, Chung-Ang University in South Korea, Georgetown University, ITESM in Mexico, Massachusetts Institute of Technology, U.S. Naval Postgraduate School, New York University, Stockholm University in Sweden, University of the Andes in Chile, University of Chile, University of Hull, University of Pennsylvania Wharton School, University of York in the United Kingdom, and Edinburgh University in Scotland, among others.

Currently a risk, finance, and economics professor, Dr. Mun has taught courses in financial management, investments, real options, economics, and statistics at the undergraduate and the graduate MS, MBA, and PhD levels. He teaches and has taught at universities all over the world, from the U.S. Naval Postgraduate School (Monterey, California) and University of Applied Sciences (Switzerland and Germany) as full professor, to Golden Gate University (California) and St. Mary's College (California), and has chaired many graduate research MBA thesis and PhD dissertation committees. He also teaches weeklong Risk Analysis, Real Options Analysis, and Risk Analysis for Managers public courses where participants can obtain the CRM and CQRM designations on completion. He is a senior fellow at the Magellan Center and sits on the board of standards at the American Academy of Financial Management.

He was formerly the Vice President of Analytics at Decisioneering, Inc., where he headed the development of options and financial analytics software products, analytical consulting, training, and technical support, and where he was the creator of the Real Options Analysis Toolkit software, the older and much less powerful predecessor of the Real Options Super Lattice software. Prior to joining Decisioneering, he was a Consulting Manager and Financial Economist in the Valuation Services and Global Financial Services practice of KPMG Consulting and a Manager with the Economic Consulting Services practice at KPMG LLP.

He has extensive experience in econometric modeling, financial analysis, real options, economic analysis, and statistics. During his tenure at Real Options Valuation, Inc., Decisioneering, and KPMG Consulting, he taught and consulted on a variety of real options, risk analysis, financial forecasting, project management, and financial valuation issues for more than 100 multinational firms (current and former clients include 3M, Airbus, Boeing, BP, Chevron Texaco, Financial Accounting Standards Board, Fujitsu, GE, Goodyear, Microsoft, Motorola, Northrop Grumman, Pfizer, Timken, U.S. Department of Defense, U.S. Navy, Veritas, and many others). His experience prior to joining KPMG included being department head of financial planning and analysis at Viking Inc. of FedEx, performing financial forecasting, economic analysis, and market research. Prior to that, he did financial planning and freelance financial consulting work.

Dr. Mun received a PhD in finance and economics from Lehigh University, where his research and academic interests were in the areas of investment finance, econometric modeling, financial options, corporate finance, and microeconomic theory. He also has an MBA in business administration, an MS in management science, and a BS in biology and physics. He is Certified in Financial Risk Management, Certified in Financial Consulting, and Certified in Quantitative Risk Management. He is a member of the American Mensa, Phi Beta Kappa Honor Society, and Golden Key Honor Society as well as several other professional organizations, including the Eastern and Southern Finance Associations, American Economic Association, and Global Association of Risk Professionals.

In addition, he has written many academic articles published in the *Journal of Expert Systems with Applications; Defense Acquisition Research Journal; American Institute of Physics Proceedings; Acquisitions Research (U.S. Department of Defense); Journal of the Advances in Quantitative Accounting and Finance; Global Finance Journal; International Financial Review; Journal of Financial Analysis; Journal of Applied Financial Economics; Journal of International Financial Markets, Institutions and Money; Financial Engineering News;* and *Journal of the Society of Petroleum Engineers.* Finally, he has contributed chapters in dozens of books and written over a hundred technical whitepapers, newsletters, case studies, and research papers for Real Options Valuation, Inc.

JohnathanMun@cs.com

San Francisco, California

ACCOLADES FOR DR. MUN'S BOOKS

...powerful toolset for portfolio/program managers to make rational choices among alternatives...
> Rear Admiral James Greene (Ret.), Acquisitions Chair
> Naval Postgraduate School (USA)

...unavoidable for any professional...logical, concrete, and conclusive approach...
> Jean Louis Vaysse, Vice President, Airbus (France)

...proven, revolutionary approach to quantifying risks and opportunities in an uncertain world...
> Mike Twyman, President, Mission Solutions,
> Cubic Global Defense, Inc. (USA)

...must read for anyone running investment economics...best way to quantify risk and strategic options...
> Mubarak A. Alkhater, Executive Director, New Business,
> Saudi Electric Co. (Saudi Arabia)

... pragmatic powerful risk techniques, valuable theoretical insights and analytics useful in any industry...
> Dr. Robert S. Finocchiaro, Director,
> Corporate R&D Services, 3M (USA)

...most important risk tools in one volume, definitive source on risk management with vivid examples...
> Dr. Ricardo Valerdi, Engineering Systems,
> Massachusetts Institute of Technology (USA)

...step-by-step complex concepts with unmatched ease and clarity... a "must read" for all professionals...
> Dr. Hans Weber, Product Development Leader,
> Syngenta AG (Switzerland)

...clear step-by-step approach...latest technology in decision making for real-world business...
> Dr. Paul W. Finnegan, Vice President, Alexion Pharmaceuticals (USA)

...clear roadmap and breadth of topics to create dynamic risk-adjusted strategies and options...
> Jeffrey A. Clark, Vice President Strategic Planning,
> The Timken Company (USA)

…clearly organized and tool-supported exploration of real-life business risks, options, strategy…

    Robert Mack, Vice President, Distinguished Analyst,
    Gartner Group (USA)

…full range of methodologies for quantifying and mitigating risk for effective enterprise management…

    Raymond Heika, Director of Strategic Planning,
    Northrop Grumman Corporation (USA)

…a must-read for product portfolio managers…captures risk exposure of strategic investments…

    Rafael Gutierrez, Executive Director Strategic Marketing Planning,
    Seagate Technologies (USA)

…complex topics exceptionally explained…
can understand and practice…

    Agustín Velázquez, Senior Economist,
    Venezuela Central Bank (Venezuela)

…constant source of practical applications with risk management theory…simply excellent!

    Alfredo Roisenzvit, Executive Director/Professor,
    Risk-Business Latin America (Argentina)

…the best risk modeling book is now better…
required reading by all executives…

    David Mercier, Vice President Corporate Dev.,
    Bonanza Creek Energy [Oil & Gas] (USA)

…bridge of theory and practice, intuitive,
understandable interpretations…

    Luis Melo, Senior Econometrician,
    Colombia Central Bank (Colombia)

…valuable tools for corporations to deliver value to shareholders and society even in rough times…

    Dr. Markus Götz Junginger, Lead Partner,
    Gallup (Germany)

CONTENTS

DISTRIBUTIONAL MOMENTS

The study of statistics refers to the collection, presentation, analysis, and utilization of numerical data to infer and make decisions in the face of uncertainty, where the actual population data is unknown. There are two branches in the study of statistics: descriptive statistics, where data is summarized and described, and inferential statistics, where the population is generalized through a small random sample, making it useful for making predictions or decisions when the population characteristics are unknown.

A *sample* can be defined as a subset of the population being measured, while the *population* can be defined as all possible observations of interest of a variable. For instance, if one is interested in the voting practices of all U.S. registered voters, the entire pool of a hundred million registered voters is considered the population while a small survey of one thousand registered voters taken from several small towns across the nation is the sample. The calculated characteristics of the sample (e.g., mean, median, standard deviation) are termed *statistics*, while *parameters* imply that the entire population has been surveyed and the results tabulated. Thus, in decision making, the statistic is of vital importance considering that sometimes the entire population is yet unknown (e.g., who are all your customers, what is the total market share, and so forth) or it is very difficult to obtain all relevant information on the population because it would be too time- or resource-consuming.

In inferential statistics, the following are the usual steps in conducting research:

- Designing the experiment—this phase includes designing the ways to collect all possible and relevant data.

    o Collection of sample data—data is gathered and tabulated

    o Analysis of data—statistical analysis is performed

    o Estimation or prediction—inferences are made based on the statistics obtained

    o Hypothesis testing—decisions are tested against the data to see the outcomes

- Determining goodness-of-fit—actual data is compared to historical data to see how accurate, valid, and reliable the inference may be.

- Decision making—decisions are made based on the outcome of the inference.

MEASURING THE CENTER OF THE DISTRIBUTION—THE FIRST MOMENT

The first moments of a distribution of outcomes measure the expected rate of return on a particular project. They measure the location of the project's scenarios and possible outcomes on average. The common statistics for the first moment include the *mean* (average), *median* (center of a distribution), and *mode* (most commonly occurring value). Figure 1.1 illustrates the first moment—where in this case, the first moment of this distribution is measured by the mean (μ) or average value.

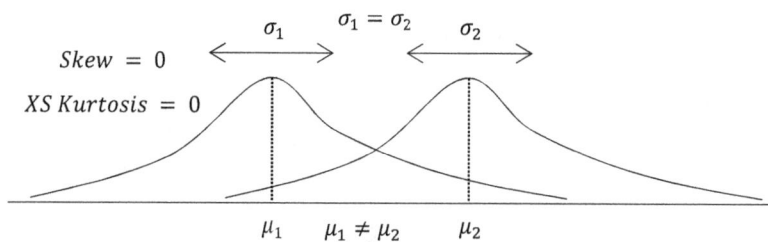

Figure 1.1: First Moment

MEASURING THE SPREAD OF THE DISTRIBUTION—THE SECOND MOMENT

The second moment measures the spread of a distribution, which is a measure of risk. The spread or width of a distribution indicates the variability of a variable, that is, the potentiality that the variable can fall into different regions of the distribution—in other words, the potential scenarios of outcomes. Figure 1.2 illustrates two distributions with identical first moments (identical means) but very different second moments or risks. The visualization becomes clearer in Figure 1.3. As an example, suppose there are two stocks and the first stock's movements (the solid line) with the smaller fluctuation is compared against the second stock's movements (the dotted line) with a much higher price fluctuation. Clearly an investor would view the stock with the wilder fluctuation as riskier because the outcomes of the riskier stock are relatively more unknown than the less risky stock. The vertical axis in Figure 1.3 measures the stock prices; thus, the riskier stock has a wider range of potential outcomes. This range is translated into a distribution's width (the horizontal axis) in Figure 1.2, where the wider distribution represents the riskier asset. Hence, width or spread of a distribution measures a variable's risks. Notice that in Figure 1.2, both distributions have identical first moments or central tendencies but clearly the distributions are very different. This difference in the distributional width is measurable. Mathematically and statistically, the width or risk of a variable can be measured through several different statistics, including the range, standard deviation (σ), variance, coefficient of variation, and percentiles.

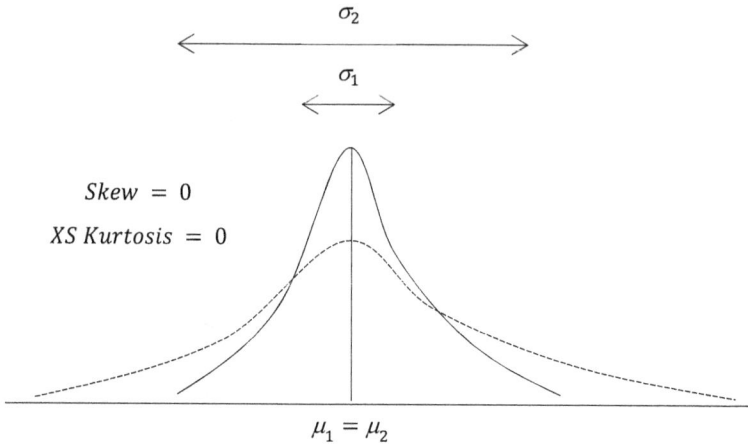

Figure 1.2: Second Moment

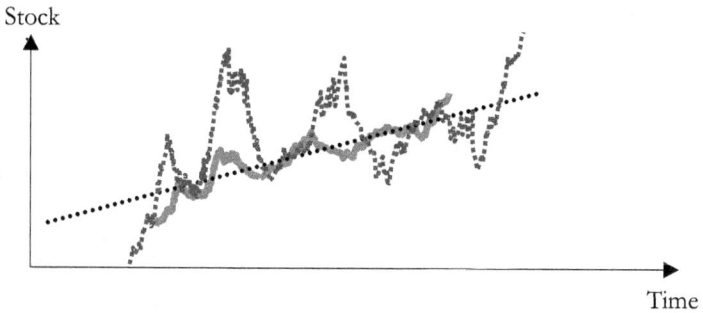

Figure 1.3: Stock Price Fluctuations

Variance and Standard Deviation

Variance and standard deviation are two common measures of the second moment. Variance is the average of the squared deviations about their means, in squared units:

$$\sigma^2 = \sum_{i=1}^{N} \frac{(x_i - \mu)^2}{N} \ and \ s^2 = \sum_{i=1}^{n} \frac{(x_i - \bar{x})^2}{n - 1}$$

Standard deviation is in original units and, thus, useful as a direct means of comparison of dispersion and variability measured in the same units:

$$\sigma = \sqrt{\sum_{i=1}^{N} \frac{(x_i - \mu)^2}{N}} \quad and \ s = \sqrt{\sum_{i=1}^{n} \frac{(x_i - \bar{x})^2}{n-1}}$$

Although standard deviation and variances have many uses, those uses are limited because their measurements are in the same units and, hence, are considered absolute values of risk.

Coefficient of Variation

The coefficient of variation (CV) is unitless and measures relative variability. It thus allows the comparison of two datasets to see which has more variability without worrying about the units. In comparison, standard deviations are absolute measures of variability and depend heavily on the data's unit of measure.

$$CV = \frac{s}{\bar{x}} \ or \ CV = \frac{\sigma}{\mu}$$

EXAMPLE

Statistic	# in family	Food expenditure ($)
$\bar{x}$	3.23	$110.5
s	1.34	$25.25

Which has more variation, the number of family members or the food expenditure?

CV in family = 1.34/3.23 = 0.415

CV in expenditures = 25.25/110.25 = 0.229

The calculations show that there is more variation in the number of family members.

MEASURING THE SKEW OF THE DISTRIBUTION—THE THIRD MOMENT

The third moment measures a distribution's skewness, that is, how the distribution is pulled to one side or the other. Figure 1.4 illustrates a negative or left skew (the tail of the distribution points to the left) and Figure 1.5 illustrates a positive or right skew (the tail of the distribution points to the right). The mean is always skewed towards the tail of the distribution, while the median remains constant. Another way of seeing this is that the mean moves but the standard deviation, variance, or width may still remain constant. If the third moment is not considered, then looking only at the expected returns (mean) and risk (standard deviation), a positively skewed project might be incorrectly chosen! For example, if the horizontal axis represents the net revenues of a project, then clearly a left or negatively skewed distribution might be preferred as there is a higher probability of greater returns (Figure 1.4) as compared to a higher probability for a lower level of returns (Figure 1.5). Thus, in a skewed distribution, the median is a better measure of returns, as the medians for both Figures 1.4 and 1.5 are identical, risks are identical, and, hence, a project with a negatively skewed distribution of net profits is a better choice. Failure to account for a project's distributional skewness may mean that the incorrect project may be chosen (e.g., two projects may have identical first and second moments, that is, they both have identical returns and risk profiles, but their distributional skews may be very different). Skew is calculated by:

$$Skew = \frac{n}{(n-1)(n-2)} \sum_{i=1}^{n} \left(\frac{x_i - \bar{x}}{s}\right)^3$$

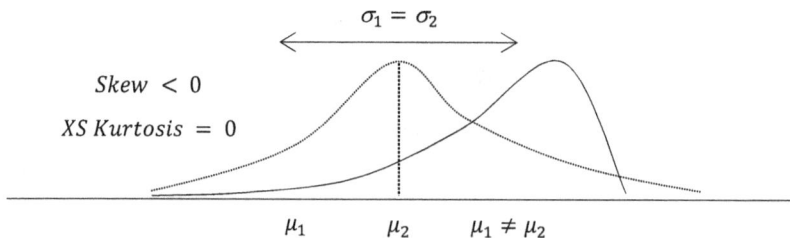

$$\sigma_1 = \sigma_2$$

Skew < 0

XS Kurtosis $= 0$

$\mu_1 \quad \mu_2 \quad \mu_1 \neq \mu_2$

Figure 1.4: Third Moment (Left Skew)

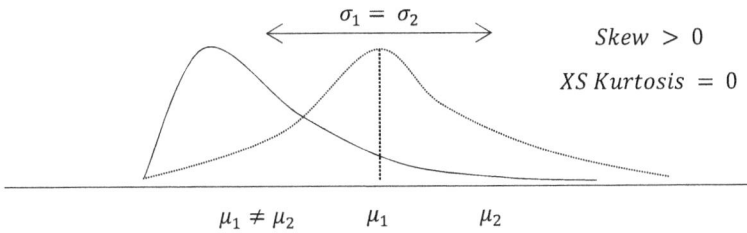

$$\sigma_1 = \sigma_2$$

$$Skew > 0$$

$$XS\ Kurtosis = 0$$

$$\mu_1 \neq \mu_2 \qquad \mu_1 \qquad \mu_2$$

Figure 1.5: Third Moment (Right Skew)

MEASURING THE CATASTROPHIC TAIL EVENTS IN A DISTRIBUTION— THE FOURTH MOMENT

The fourth moment, or kurtosis, measures the peakedness of a distribution. Figure 1.6 illustrates this effect. The background is a normal distribution with a kurtosis of 3.0 or an excess kurtosis of 0 (XS kurtosis is defined as the kurtosis difference from a normal distribution). The new distribution has a higher kurtosis, thus the area under the curve is thicker at the tails with less area in the central body. This condition has major impacts on uncertainty analysis because for the two distributions in Figure 1.6, the first three moments (mean, standard deviation, and skewness) can be identical but the fourth moment (kurtosis) is different. This means that although the expected returns and uncertainties are identical, the probabilities of extreme and catastrophic events (potential large losses or large gains) occurring are higher for a high kurtosis distribution (e.g., stock market returns are leptokurtic or have high kurtosis). Ignoring a project's return's kurtosis may be detrimental. Kurtosis is defined as:

$$Kurtosis = \frac{n(n+1)}{(n-1)(n-2)(n-3)} \sum_{i=1}^{n} \left(\frac{x_i - \bar{x}}{s} \right)^4 - \frac{3(n-1)^2}{(n-2)(n-3)}$$

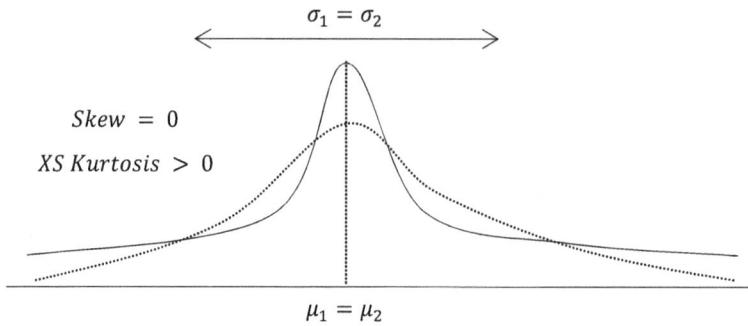

$$\sigma_1 = \sigma_2$$

$$Skew = 0$$

$$XS\ Kurtosis > 0$$

$$\mu_1 = \mu_2$$

Figure 1.6: Fourth Moment

Most distributions can be defined by up to four moments. The first moment describes a distribution's location or central tendency (expected value); the second moment describes its width or spread (uncertainty); the third moment, its directional skew (most probable events); and the fourth moment, its peakedness or thickness in the tails (catastrophic extreme tail events). All four moments should be calculated and interpreted to provide a more comprehensive view of the project under analysis.

2

THE BASICS OF INTERPRETING PDF, CDF, AND ICDF CHARTS

This chapter briefly explains the probability density function (PDF) for continuous distributions, which is also called the probability mass function (PMF) for discrete distributions (we use these terms interchangeably), where given some distribution and its parameters, we can determine the probability of occurrence given some outcome or random variable x. In addition, the cumulative distribution function (CDF) can also be computed, which is the sum of the PDF values up to this x value. Finally, the inverse cumulative distribution function (ICDF) is used to compute the value x given the cumulative probability of occurrence.

In mathematics and Monte Carlo risk simulation, a probability density function (PDF) represents a continuous probability distribution in terms of integrals. If a probability distribution has a density of $f(x)$, then, intuitively, the infinitesimal interval of $[x, x + dx]$ has a probability of $f(x)dx$. The PDF, therefore, can be seen as a smoothed version of a probability histogram; that is, by providing an empirically large sample of a continuous random variable repeatedly, the histogram using very narrow ranges will resemble the random variable's PDF. The probability of the interval between $[a, b]$ is given by $\int_a^b f(x)dx$, which means that the total integral of the function f must be 1.0.

It is a common mistake to incorrectly think of $f(a)$ as the probability of a. In fact, $f(a)$ can sometimes be larger than 1 (consider a uniform distribution between 0.0 and 0.5). The random variable x

within this distribution will have $f(x)$ greater than 1. The probability, in reality, is the function $f(x)dx$ discussed previously, where dx is an infinitesimal amount.

The cumulative distribution function (CDF) is denoted as $F(x) = P(X \leq x)$, indicating the probability of X taking on a less than or equal value to x. Every CDF is monotonically increasing, is continuous from the right, and at the limits has the following properties: $\lim_{x \to -\infty} F(x) = 0$ and $\lim_{x \to +\infty} F(x) = 1$.

Further, the CDF is related to the PDF by $F(b) - F(a) = P(a \leq X \leq b) = \int_a^b f(x)dx$, where the PDF function f is the derivative of the CDF function F. In probability theory, a probability mass function, or PMF, gives the probability that a discrete random variable is exactly equal to some value. The PMF differs from the PDF in that the values of the latter, defined only for continuous random variables, are not probabilities; rather, its integral over a set of possible values of the random variable is a probability. A random variable is discrete if its probability distribution is discrete and can be characterized by a PMF.

Therefore, X is a discrete random variable if

$$\sum_u P(X = u) = 1$$

as u runs through all possible values of the random variable X.

INTERPRETING PROBABILITY CHARTS

Here are some tips to help decipher the characteristics of a distribution when looking at different PDF and CDF charts:

- For each distribution, a continuous distribution's PDF is shown as an area chart (Figure 2.1) whereas a discrete distribution's PMF is shown as a bar chart (Figure 2.2).

- If the distribution can only take a single shape (e.g., normal distributions are always bell shaped, with the only difference being the central tendency measured by the mean and the spread measured by the standard deviation), then typically only one PDF area chart will be shown with an overlay PDF line chart (Figure 2.3) showing the effects of various parameters on the distribution.

- The CDF charts, or S-Curves, are shown as line charts (Figure 2.4), and sometimes as bar graphs.

- The central tendency of a distribution (e.g., the mean of a normal distribution) is its central location (Figure 2.3).

- Multiple area charts and line charts will be shown (e.g., beta distribution) if the distribution can take on multiple shapes (e.g., the beta distribution is a uniform distribution when alpha = beta = 1; a parabolic distribution when alpha = beta = 2; a triangular distribution when alpha = 1 and beta = 2, or vice versa; a positively skewed distribution when alpha = 2 and beta = 5, and so forth). In this case, you will see multiple area charts and line charts (Figure 2.5).

- The starting point of the distribution is sometimes its minimum parameter (e.g., parabolic, triangular, uniform, arcsine, etc.) or its location parameter (e.g., the beta distribution's starting location is 0, but a beta 4 distribution's starting point is the location parameter; Figure 2.5 shows a beta 4 distribution with location = 10, its starting point on the x-axis).

- The ending point of the distribution is sometimes its maximum parameter (e.g., parabolic, triangular, uniform, arcsine, etc.) or its natural maximum multiplied by the factor parameter shifted by a location parameter (e.g., the original beta distribution has a minimum of 0 and maximum value of 1, but a beta 4 distribution with location = 10 and factor = 2 indicates that the shifted starting point is 10 and ending point is 11, and its width of 1 is multiplied by a factor of 2, which means that the beta 4 distribution now will have an ending value of 12, as shown in Figure 2.5).

- Interactions between parameters are sometimes evident. For example, in the beta 4 distribution, if the alpha = beta, the distribution is symmetrical, whereas it is more positively skewed the greater the difference between beta and alpha, and the more negatively skewed, the greater the difference between alpha and beta (Figure 2.6).

- Sometimes a distribution's PDF is shaped by two or three parameters called *shape*, *scale*, and *location*. For instance, the Laplace distribution has two input parameters, alpha location and beta scale, where alpha indicates the central tendency of the distribution (like the mean in a normal distribution) and beta indicates the spread from the mean (like the standard deviation in a normal distribution).

- The narrower the PDF (Figure 2.3's normal distribution with a mean of 10 and standard deviation of 2), the steeper the CDF S-Curve looks (Figure 2.4), and the smaller the width on the CDF curve.

- A 45-degree straight line CDF (an imaginary straight line connecting the starting and ending points of the CDF) indicates a uniform distribution; an S-Curve CDF with equal amounts above and below the 45-degree straight line indicates a symmetrical and somewhat bell- or mound-shaped curve; a CDF completely curved above the 45-degree line indicates a positively skewed distribution (Figure 2.7), while a CDF completely curved below the 45-degree line indicates a negatively skewed distribution (Figure 2.8).

- A CDF line that looks identical in shape but shifted to the right or left indicates the same distribution but shifted by some location, and a CDF line that starts from the same point but is pulled both to the left and right indicates a multiplicative effect on the distribution such as a factor multiplication, as shown in Figures 2.9 and 2.10.

- An almost vertical CDF indicates a high kurtosis distribution with fat tails, and where the center of the distribution is pulled up (e.g., see the Cauchy distribution) versus a relatively flat CDF, a very wide and perhaps flat-tailed distribution is indicated.

- Some discrete distributions can be approximated by a continuous distribution if its number of trials is sufficiently large and its probability of success and failure is fairly symmetrical (e.g., see the binomial and negative binomial distributions). For instance, with a small number of trials and a low probability of success, the binomial distribution is positively skewed, whereas it approaches a symmetrical normal distribution when the number of trials is high and the probability of success is around 0.50.

- Many distributions are both flexible and interchangeable— refer to the details of each distribution in Chapter 4 and 5

Appendices—e.g., binomial is Bernoulli repeated multiple times; arcsine and parabolic are special cases of beta; Pascal is a shifted negative binomial; binomial and Poisson approach normal at the limit; chi-square is the squared sum of multiple normal; Erlang is a special case of gamma; exponential is the inverse of the Poisson but on a continuous basis; F is the ratio of two chi-squares; gamma is related to the lognormal, exponential, Pascal, Erlang, Poisson, and chi-square distributions; Laplace comprises two exponential distributions in one; the log of a lognormal approaches normal; the sum of multiple discrete uniforms approach normal; Pearson V is the inverse of gamma; Pearson VI is the ratio of two gammas; PERT is a modified beta; a large degree of freedom T approaches normal; Rayleigh is a modified Weibull; and so forth.

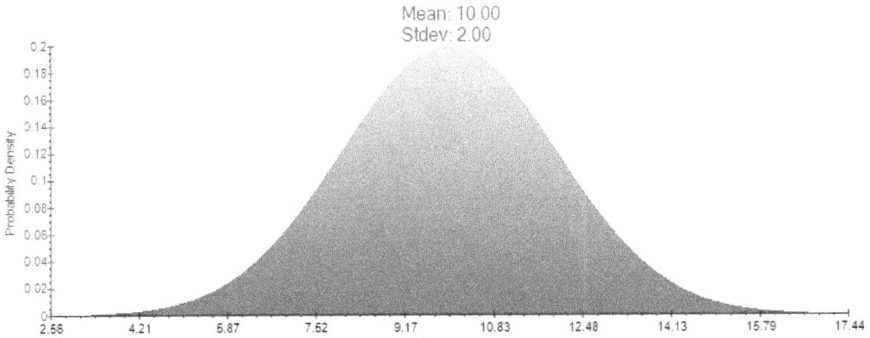

Figure 2.1: Continuous PDF (Area Chart)

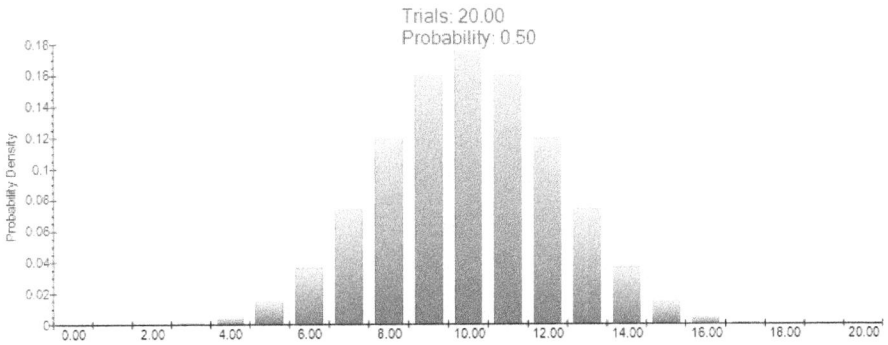

Figure 2.2: Discrete PMF (Bar Chart)

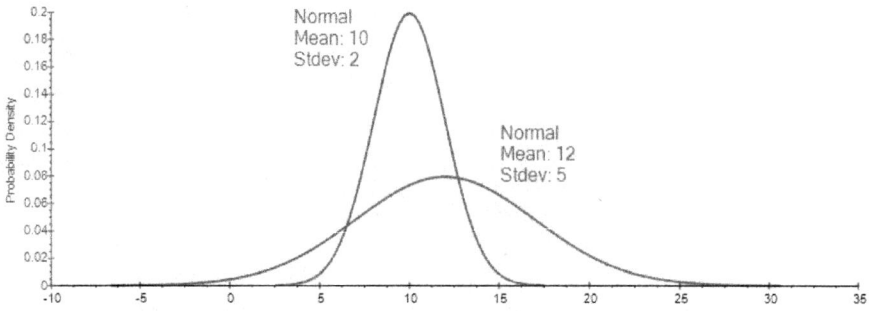

Figure 2.3: Multiple Continuous PDF Overlay Charts

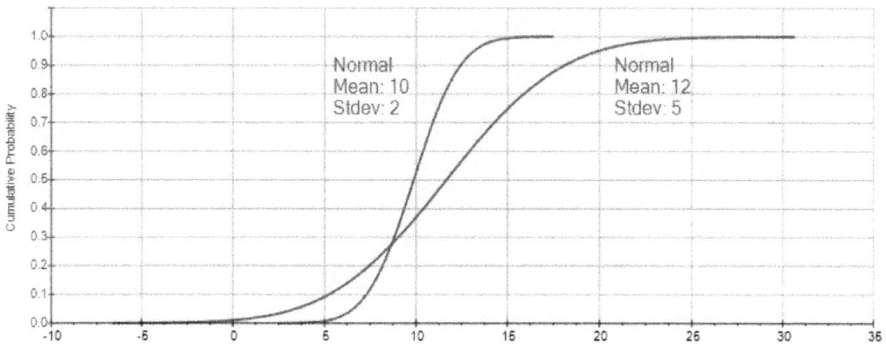

Figure 2.4: CDF Overlay Charts

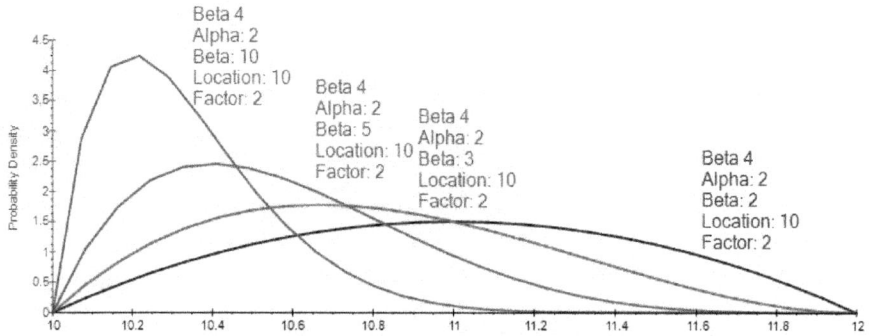

Figure 2.5: PDF Characteristics of the Beta Distribution

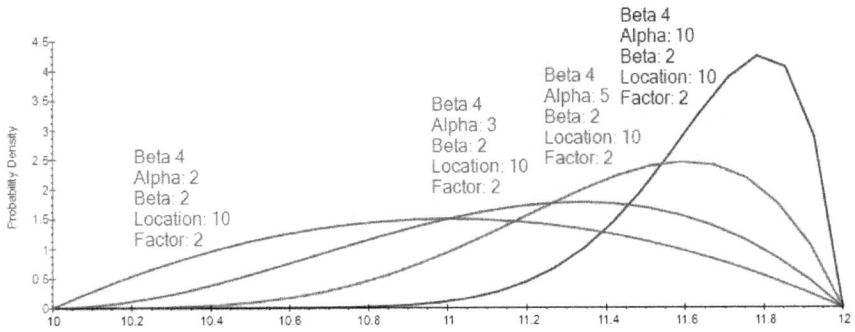

Figure 2.6: PDF of a Negatively Skewed Beta Distribution

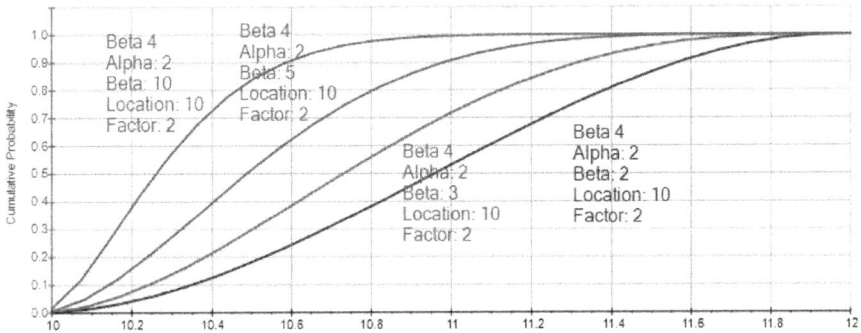

Figure 2.7: CDF of a Positively Skewed Distribution

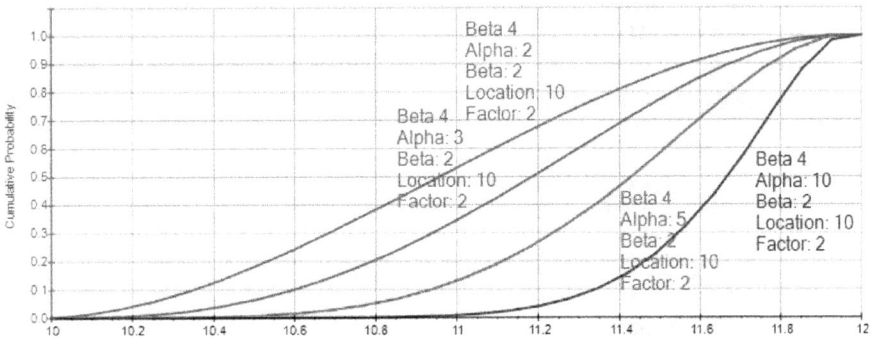

Figure 2.8: CDF of a Negatively Skewed Distribution

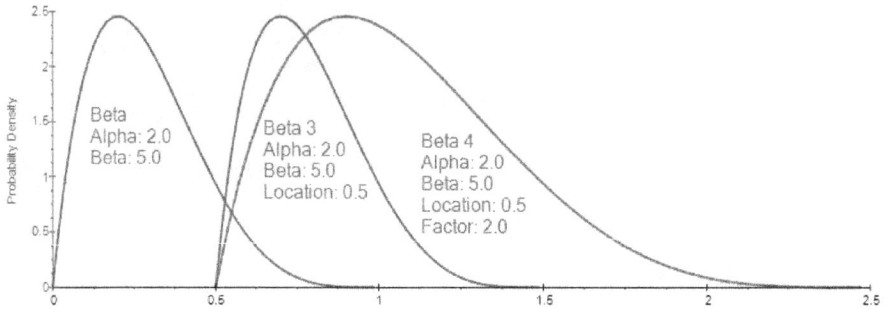

Figure 2.9: PDF Characteristics of a Shift

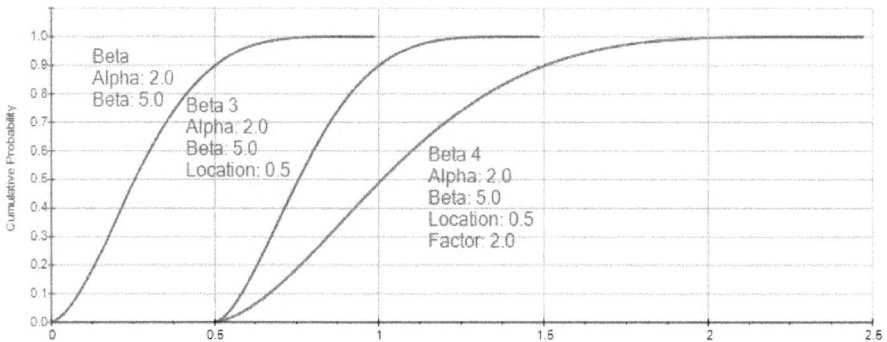

Figure 2.10: CDF Characteristics of a Shift

Distributional Charts and Tables is a new Probability Distribution tool that is a very powerful and fast module used for generating distribution charts and tables. Note that there are three similar tools in Risk Simulator but each does very different things:

1. Distributional Analysis: Used to quickly compute the PDF, CDF, and ICDF of the 50 probability distributions available in Risk Simulator, and to return a probability table of these values.

2. Distributional Charts and Tables: The Probability Distribution tool described here used to compare different parameters of the same distribution (e.g., the shapes and PDF, CDF, ICDF values of a Weibull distribution with Alpha and Beta of [2, 2], [3, 5], and [3.5, 8], and overlays them on top of one another).

3. Overlay Charts: Used to compare different distributions (theo-
    retical input assumptions and empirically simulated output
    forecasts) and to overlay them on top of one another for a visual
    comparison.

SHAPES OF DISTRIBUTIONS

The following illustrates how multiple probability distribution charts
can be developed and compared against each other.

*   Run *Risk Simulator | Analytical Tools | Distributional Charts and
    Tables,* click on the *Apply Global Inputs* button to load a sam-
    ple set of input parameters or enter your own inputs, and
    click *Run* to compute the results. The resulting four mo-
    ments and CDF, ICDF, PDF are computed for each of the
    50 probability distributions (Figure 2.11).

*   Click on the *Charts and Tables* tab (Figure 2.12), select a dis-
    tribution (e.g., Beta 4), then choose if you wish to run the
    CDF, ICDF, or PDF, enter the relevant inputs, and click
    Run Chart. You can switch between the *Chart* and *Table* tab
    to view the results as well as try out some of the chart icons
    to see the effects on the chart.

*   You can also change two parameters to generate multiple
    charts and distribution tables by entering the *From | To |
    Step* input after selecting the relevant *Change First* and *Second
    Parameter* droplists; then hit *Run.* For example, as illustrated
    in Figure 2.12, run the Beta 4 distribution and select PDF,
    select *Alpha* and *Beta* to change using the custom droplists
    and enter the relevant input parameters: 3; 5; 2 for the Alpha
    inputs and 2; 4; 2 for the Beta inputs, and click *Run Chart.*
    This will generate four Beta 4 distributions: Beta 4 (3, 2, 10,
    2), Beta 4 (3, 4, 10, 2), Beta 4 (5, 2, 10, 2), and Beta 4 (5, 4,
    10, 2). Explore various chart types, gridlines, language, and
    decimal settings, and try rerunning the distribution using
    theoretical versus empirically simulated values.

*   Figure 2.13 is the same set of distributions viewed under the
    CDF selection with gridlines turned on. Notice that the dec-
    imal has been set to 1 and the labels have been moved to
    different locations for the sake of clarity of the charts. Use
    the *Index* number droplist (default is 1) and +A, –A, ←A,

→A, A↑, and A↓ icons (located immediately above the chart) to resize and move the labels. The index droplist is used to select which chart line's labels you wish to manipulate.

- Figure 2.14 illustrates the probability tables generated for a binomial distribution where the probability of success and number of successful trials (random variable X) are selected to vary using the *From | To | Step* option. Try to replicate the calculation as shown and click on the *Table* tab to view the created CDF results. This example uses a binomial distribution with a starting input set of *Trials* = 20, *Probability* (i.e., the probability of success for each trial) = 0.5, and *Random X* (the number of successful trials) = 10, where the *Probability* is allowed to change from 0.1, 0.2, ..., 0.9 and is shown as the row variable, and the *Number of Successful Trials* is also allowed to change from 0, 1, 2, ..., 20, and is shown as the column variable. CDF is chosen and, hence, the results in the table show the cumulative probability given that the number of successful events occurs under various probabilities of success.

- Finally, Figure 2.15 shows the *Compare Charts* subtab where PDF and CDF curves from different probability distributions can be overlaid on top of one another to compare their characteristics. The example shown has the PDFs of the gamma and Weibull distributions. Start by going to the *Charts and Tables | Compare Charts* subtab and select the *Weibull* distribution. Enter *Alpha* = 2 and *Beta* = 5 and click *Add.* Then, select the *Gamma* distribution and enter the same alpha and beta values, and click *Add.* Finally, click *Run Chart* to see the resulting distributions.

Figure 2.16 illustrates the complex interrelationships among the various distributions described above. Some distributions are simply special cases of other distributions (e.g., standard-normal distribution is a special case of the normal distribution), limiting cases (e.g., the t-distribution approaches the normal distribution at the limit), modifications of others (e.g., power 3 is a modification of the power distribution by adding a location and multiplicative factor parameter), and mathematical transformations (e.g., log gamma is a logarithmic transformation of the gamma distribution). In other cases, some distributions can be obtained through a mathematical convolution of multiple identical distributions (e.g., the sum of uniform distributions converges to the normal distribution) or different distributions (e.g., the division of two different chi-square distributions approaches the F-distribution). Therefore, newer and more complex distributions can be developed using these basic building blocks. However, it is mathematically complex to create or model new distributions analytically, but, by using Monte Carlo risk simulation methods, new and unique distributions can be readily and easily created by simply adding, subtracting, multiplying, dividing, and applying any other combinations of mathematical operators among multiple simulation assumptions to generate your own unique probability distribution, without the need for complex mathematics.

ROV PROBABILITY DISTRIBUTIONS

Distributions | Charts and Tables

This tool lists all the probability distributions available in Real Options Valuation, Inc.'s suite of products.

Apply Global Inputs

Minimum	10	Alpha	2	Location	10	Percentile	0.5
Maximum	20	Beta	5	Probability	0.5	DF	10
Most Likely	15	Lambda	1.2	Factor	2	Trials	20

Mean	10	Alpha 1	5	DF Numerator	10
Stdev	2	Alpha 2	5	DF Denominator	20
Successes	5	Population	100	Pop Success	50

Arcsine
Minimum 10
Maximum 20
Random X 12
Percentile 0.5
PDF 0.7938
CDF 0.2952
ICDF 15.0000
Mean 15.0000
Stdev 3.5355
Skew 0.0000
Kurtosis -1.5000

Bernoulli
Probability 0.5
Random X 0
Percentile 0.5
PDF 0.5000
CDF 0.5000
ICDF 1.0000
Mean 0.5000
Stdev 0.5000
Skew 0.0000
Kurtosis -2.0000

Beta
Alpha 2
Beta 5
Random X 0.6
Percentile 0.5
PDF 0.4608
CDF 0.9590
ICDF 0.2644
Mean 0.2857
Stdev 0.1597
Skew 0.5963
Kurtosis -0.1200

Beta 3
Alpha 2
Beta 5
Location 10
Random X 10.25
Percentile 0.5
PDF 2.3730
CDF 0.4461
ICDF 10.2644
Mean 10.2857
Stdev 0.1597
Skew 0.5963
Kurtosis -0.1200

Beta 4
Alpha 5
Beta 5
Location 10
Factor
Random X 10.8
Percentile 0.5
PDF 1.5552
CDF 0.7667
ICDF 10.5289
Mean 10.5714
Stdev 0.3194
Skew 0.5963
Kurtosis -0.1200

Binomial
Trials 20
Probability 0.5
Random X 10
Percentile 0.5
PDF 0.1762
CDF 0.5881
ICDF 10.0000
Mean 10.0000

Cauchy
Alpha 2
Beta 5
Random X 12
Percentile 0.5
PDF 0.0127
CDF 0.8524
ICDF 2.0000

Chi-Square
DF 10
Random X 14
Percentile 0.5
PDF 0.0456
CDF 0.8270
ICDF 9.3418
Mean 10.0000

Cosine
Minimum 10
Maximum 20
Random X 15.5
Percentile 0.5
PDF 0.1551
CDF 0.5782
ICDF 15.0000
Mean 15.0000

Discrete Uniform
Minimum 10
Maximum 20
Random X 16
Percentile 0.5
PDF 0.0909
CDF 0.6364
ICDF 15.0000
Mean 15.0000

Decimals: 4   Language: English   Run   Close

Figure 2.11: Distributional Charts and Tables Tool

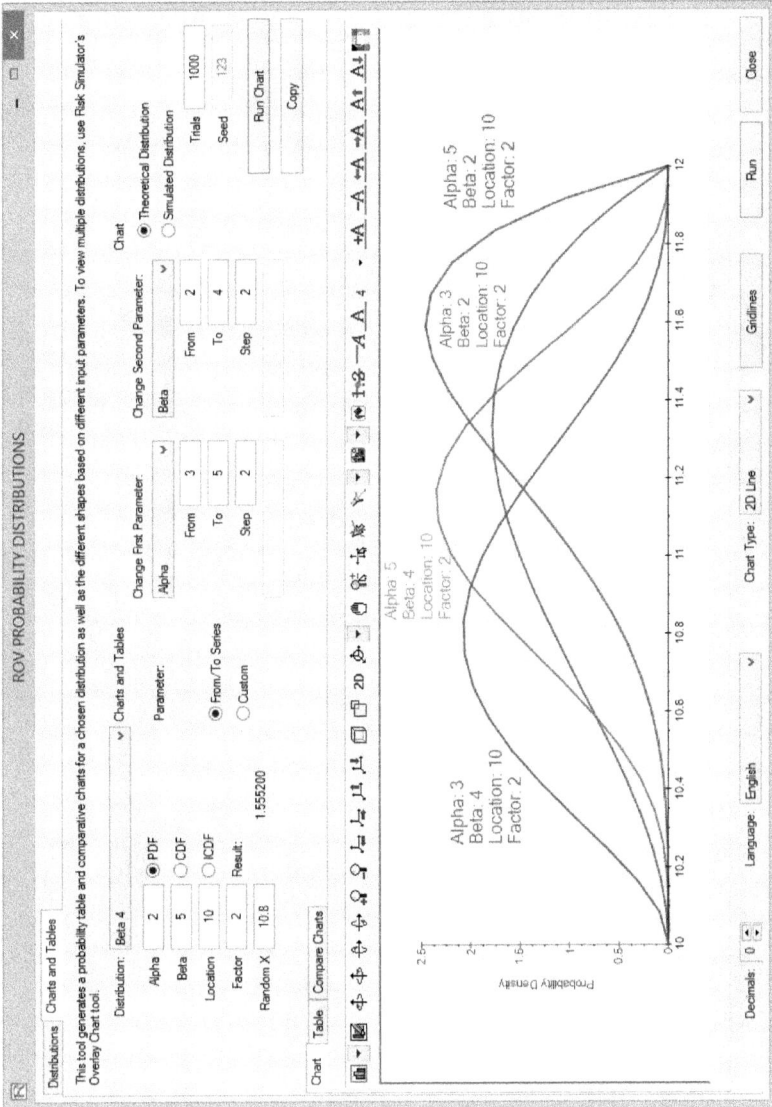

Figure 2.12: Overlaying Multiple PDF Charts

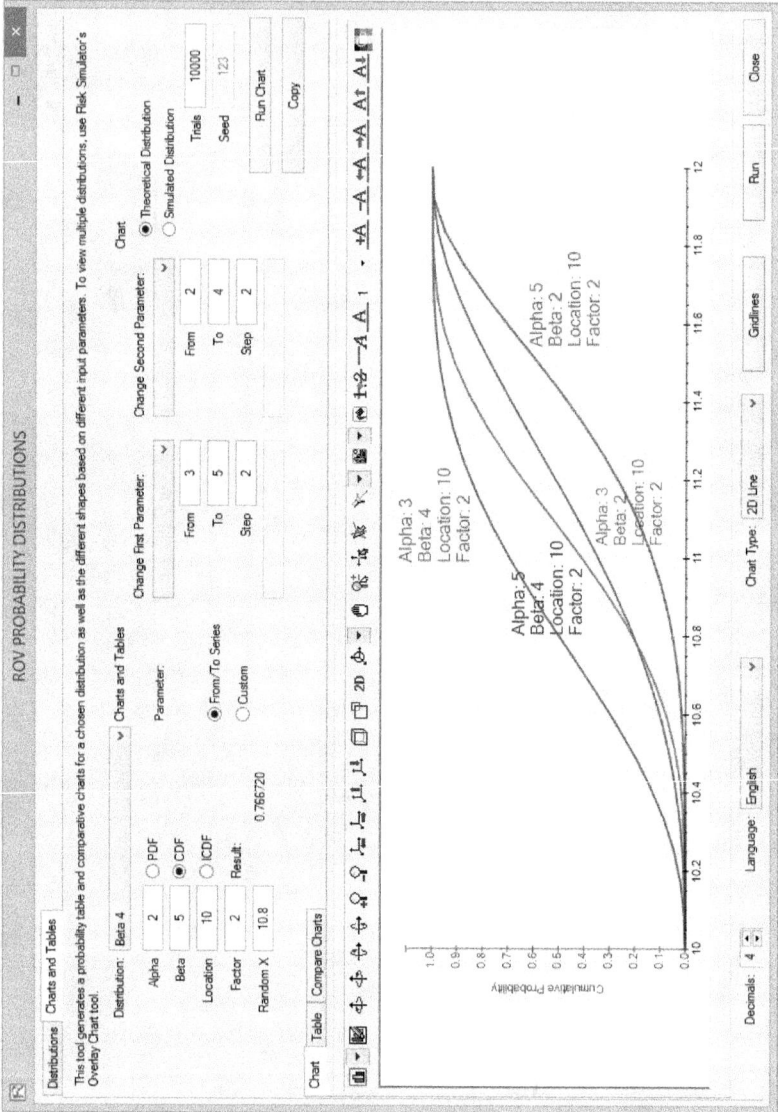

Figure 2.13: Overlay CDF Charts with Gridlines

ROV PROBABILITY DISTRIBUTIONS

Distributions | Charts and Tables

This tool generates a probability table and comparative charts for a chosen distribution as well as the different shapes based on different input parameters. To view multiple distributions, use Risk Simulator's Overlay Chart tool.

Distribution: Binomial

- Trials: 20
- Probability: 0.5
- Random X: 10
- Result: 0.888099

○ PDF ● CDF ○ ICDF

Charts and Tables

Parameter: ● From/To Series ○ Custom

Change First Parameter: Random X — From 0, To 20, Step 1

Change Second Parameter: Probability — From 0.1, To 0.9, Step 0.1

Chart: ● Theoretical Distribution ○ Simulated Distribution — Trials 1000, Seed 123

Run Table | Copy

Chart | Table | Compare Charts

Row Variable: Random X Column Variable: Probability Type: CDF

N		0.1000	0.2000	0.3000	0.4000	0.5000	0.6000	0.7000	0.8000	0.9000
1	0.0000	0.1216	0.0115	0.0008	0.0000	0.0000	0.0000	0.0000	0.0000	0.0000
2	1.0000	0.3917	0.0692	0.0076	0.0005	0.0000	0.0000	0.0000	0.0000	0.0000
3	2.0000	0.6769	0.2061	0.0355	0.0036	0.0002	0.0000	0.0000	0.0000	0.0000
4	3.0000	0.8670	0.4114	0.1071	0.0160	0.0013	0.0000	0.0000	0.0000	0.0000
5	4.0000	0.9568	0.6296	0.2375	0.0510	0.0059	0.0003	0.0000	0.0000	0.0000
6	5.0000	0.9887	0.8042	0.4164	0.1256	0.0207	0.0016	0.0000	0.0000	0.0000
7	6.0000	0.9976	0.9133	0.6080	0.2500	0.0577	0.0065	0.0003	0.0000	0.0000
8	7.0000	0.9996	0.9679	0.7723	0.4159	0.1316	0.0210	0.0013	0.0001	0.0000
9	8.0000	0.9999	0.9900	0.8867	0.5956	0.2517	0.0565	0.0051	0.0006	0.0000
10	9.0000	1.0000	0.9974	0.9520	0.7553	0.4119	0.1275	0.0171	0.0026	0.0000
11	10.0000	1.0000	0.9994	0.9829	0.8725	0.5881	0.2447	0.0480	0.0100	0.0001
12	11.0000	1.0000	0.9999	0.9949	0.9435	0.7483	0.4044	0.1133	0.0321	0.0004
13	12.0000	1.0000	1.0000	0.9987	0.9790	0.8684	0.5841	0.2277	0.0867	0.0024
14	13.0000	1.0000	1.0000	0.9997	0.9935	0.9423	0.7500	0.3920	0.0867	0.0024

Decimals: 4 Language: English

Run | Close

Figure 2.14: Probability Tables

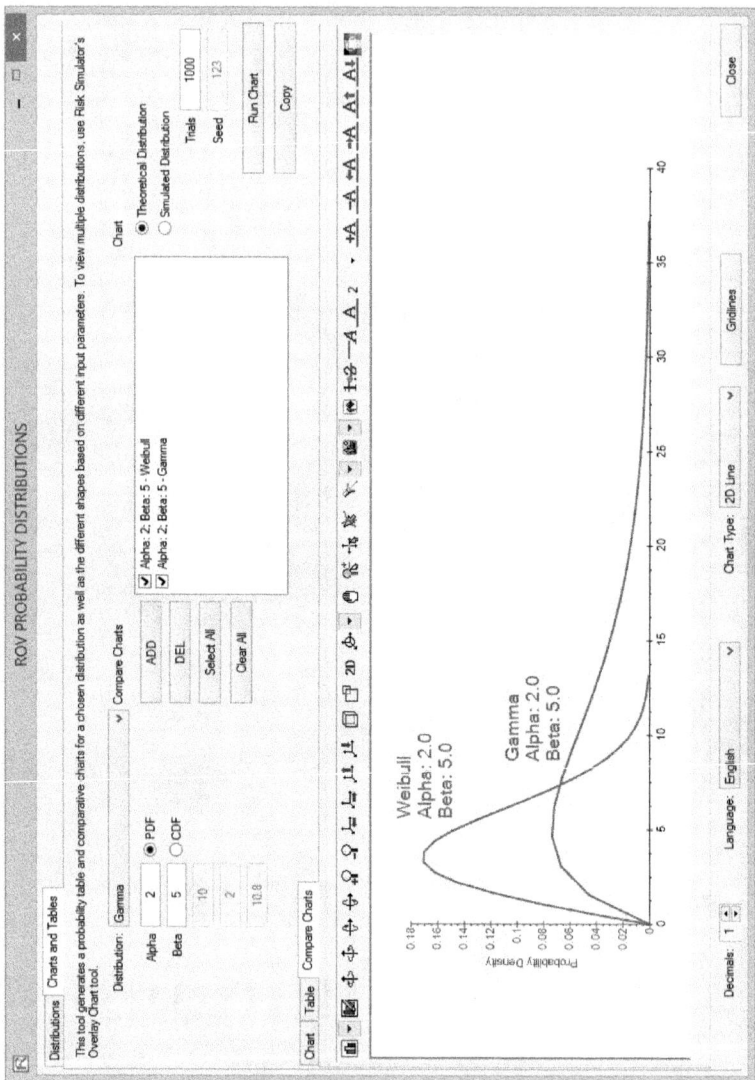

Figure 2.15: Overlay and Compare Different Distributions

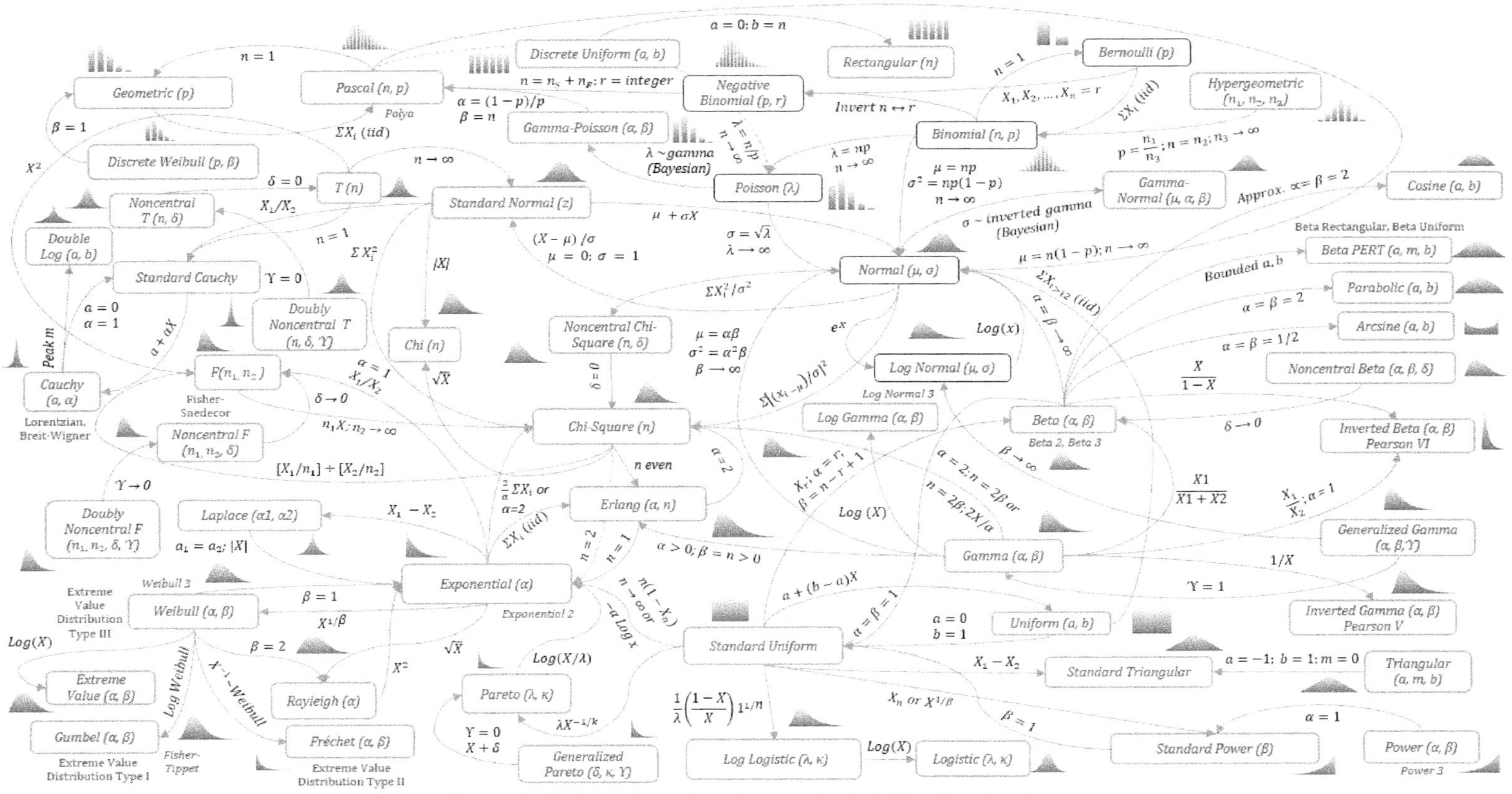

Figure 2.16: Relationships Among Probability Distributions

3

PROBABILITY DISTRIBUTION ANALYSIS TOOL

The distributional analysis tool is a statistical probability tool in Risk Simulator that is useful in a variety of settings. It can be used to compute the probability density function (PDF), which is also called the probability mass function (PMF) for discrete distributions (these terms are used interchangeably), where given some distribution and its parameters, we can determine the probability of occurrence given some outcome x. In addition, the cumulative distribution function (CDF) can be computed, which is the sum of the PDF values up to this x value. Finally, the inverse cumulative distribution function (ICDF) is used to compute the value x given the cumulative probability of occurrence. The following pages provide example uses of PDF, CDF, and ICDF. Also remember to try some of the examples throughout this book for more hands-on applications of probability distribution analysis using this tool.

This tool is accessible via *Risk Simulator | Analytical Tools | Distributional Analysis*. As an example of its use, Figure 3.1 shows the computation of a binomial distribution (i.e., a distribution with two outcomes, such as the tossing of a coin, where the outcome is either Heads or Tails, with some prescribed probability of heads and tails). Suppose we toss a coin two times and set the outcome Heads as a success. We use the binomial distribution with Trials = 2 (tossing the coin twice) and Probability = 0.50 (the probability of success, of getting Heads). Selecting the PDF and setting the range of values x as from 0 to 2 with a step size of 1 (this means we are requesting the values 0, 1, 2 for x), the resulting probabilities are provided in the table and in a graphic format, as well as the theoretical four moments of the distribution. As the outcomes of the coin toss is Heads-Heads, Tails-Tails, Heads-Tails, and Tails-Heads, the probability of getting exactly no Heads is 25%, of getting one Heads is 50%, and of getting two Heads is 25%.

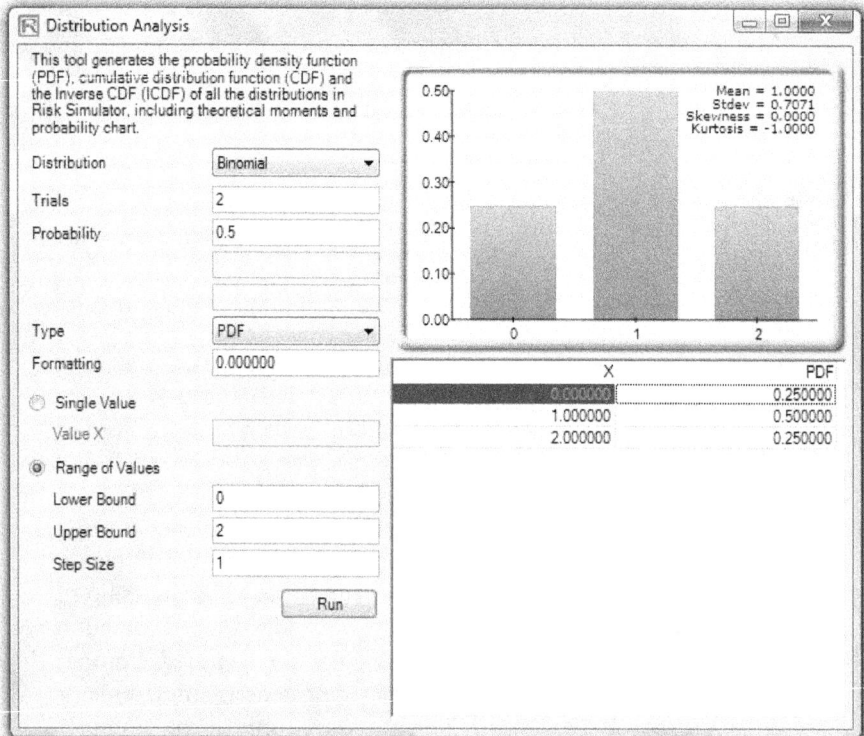

Figure 3.1: Distributional Analysis Tool (Binomial with 2 Trials)

Similarly, we can obtain the exact probabilities of tossing the coin, say 20 times, as seen in Figure 3.2. The results are again presented both in tabular and graphic formats. As a side note, the binomial distribution describes the number of times a particular event occurs in a fixed number of trials, such as the number of heads in 10 flips of a coin or the number of defective items out of 50 items chosen. The three conditions underlying the binomial distribution are:

- For each trial, only two outcomes are possible that are mutually exclusive.

- The trials are independent—what happens in the first trial does not affect the next trial.

- The probability of an event occurring remains the same from trial to trial.

The probability of success (*p*) and the integer number of total trials (*n*) are the distributional parameters. The number of successful trials is denoted *x*. It is important to note that probability of success (*p*) of 0 or 1 are trivial conditions and do not require any simulations, and, hence, are not allowed in the software.

Input requirements:

$0 < $ *Probability of success* $ < 1$ (that is, $0.0001 \leq p \leq 0.9999$)

$1 \leq$ *Number of trials* ≤ 1000 positive integers (for larger trials, use the normal distribution with the relevant computed binomial mean and standard deviation as the normal distribution's parameters)

Figure 3.3 shows the same binomial distribution but now the CDF is computed. The CDF is simply the sum of the PDF values up to the point *x*. For instance, in Figure 3.2, we see that the probabilities of 0, 1, and 2 are 0.000001, 0.000019, and 0.000181, whose sum is 0.000201, which is the value of the CDF at $x = 2$ in Figure 3.3. Whereas the PDF computes the probabilities of getting exactly 2 Heads, the CDF computes the probability of getting no more than 2 Heads or up to 2 Heads (or probabilities of 0, 1, and 2 Heads). Taking the complement (i.e., $1 - 0.00021$) obtains 0.999799, or 99.9799%, which is the probability of getting at least 3 Heads or more.

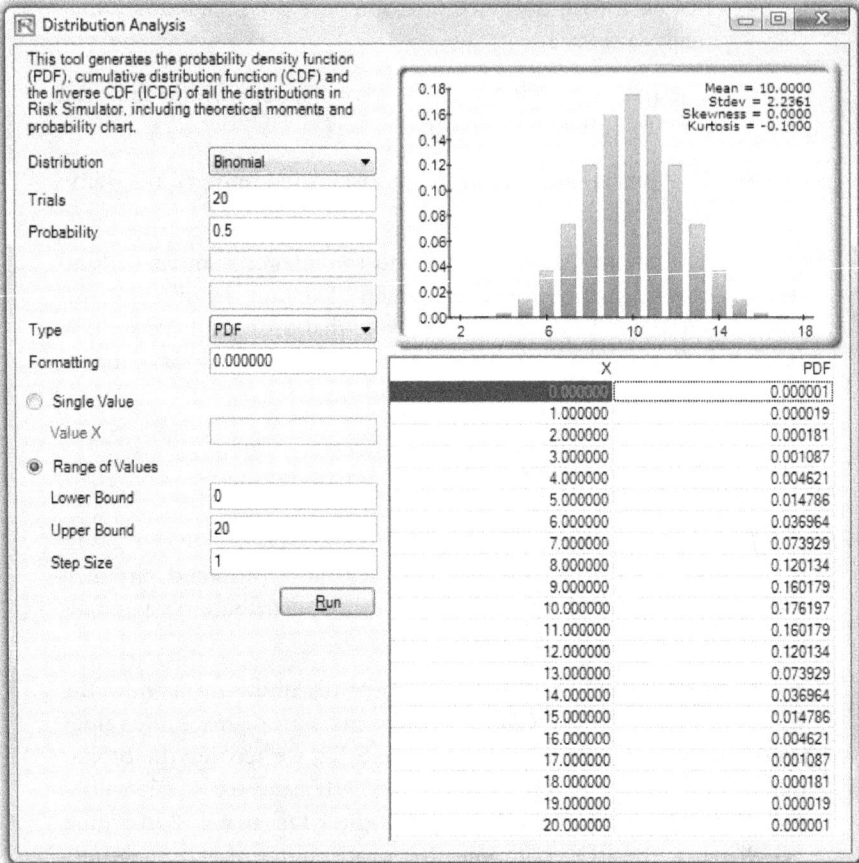

Figure 3.2: Distributional Analysis Tool (Binomial with 20 Trials)

As another example, out of 20 projects where there is a 50% independent chance of success of each project, the probability of getting at least 8 successful projects is 86.84% (i.e., the sum of the probabilities of exactly 8, 9, 10, …, 20 successful projects or 100% – the cumulative probability of 0 to 7 from Figure 3.3, or 100% – 13.16% = 86.84%). Alternatively, out of 20 independent projects, the probability of having no more than 12 successful projects is 86.84% (CDF of 12 is 86.84% in Figure 3.3). The probability in this example is the same due to the 50% success probability in a binomial distribution, which creates a symmetrical distribution (8 failures is the same as 12 successes out of 20 projects).

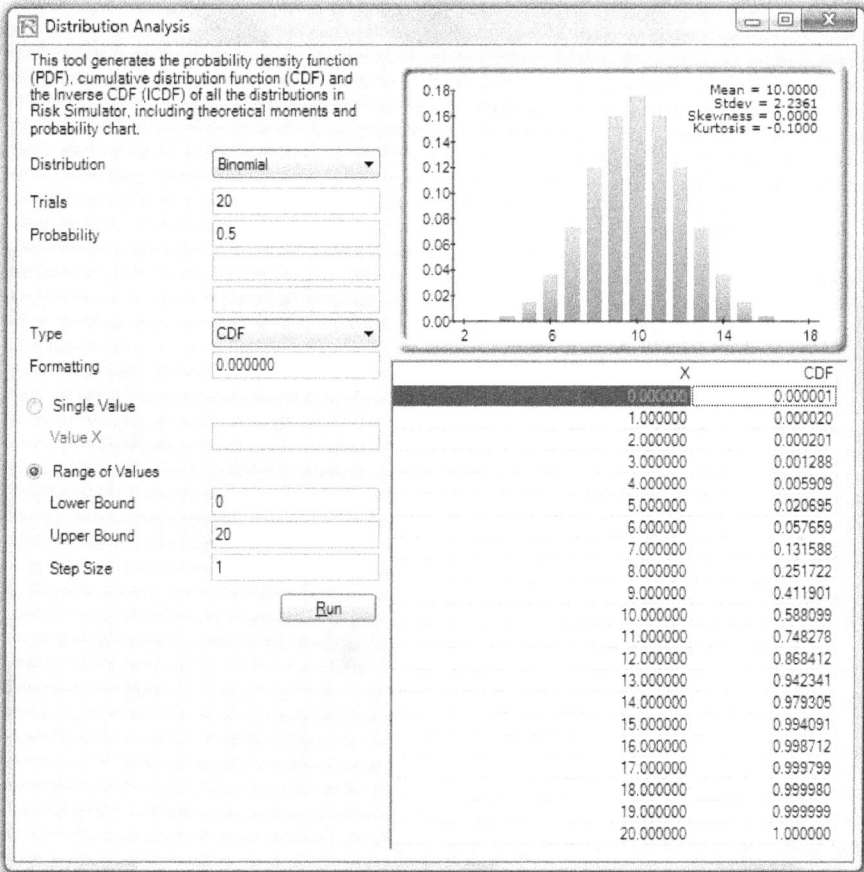

Figure 3.3: Distributional Analysis Tool (Binomial CDF with 20 Trials)

Using this distributional analysis tool, distributions even more advanced can be analyzed, such as the gamma, beta, negative binomial, and many others in Risk Simulator. As a further example of the tool's use in a continuous distribution and the ICDF functionality, Figure 3.4 shows the standard-normal distribution (normal distribution with a mean or *mu* of zero and standard deviation or *sigma* of one), where we apply the ICDF to find the value of *x* that corresponds to the cumulative probability of 97.50% (CDF). That is, a one-tail CDF of 97.50% is equivalent to a two-tail 95% confidence interval (there is a 2.50% probability in the right tail and 2.50% in the left tail, leaving 95% in the center or confidence interval area, which is equivalent to a 97.50% area for one tail). The result is the familiar Z-Score of 1.96. Therefore, using this distributional analysis tool, the standardized scores for other distributions and the exact and cumulative probabilities of other distributions can all be obtained quickly and easily. See the exercises throughout this book for more hands-on applications using the binomial, negative binomial, and other distributions.

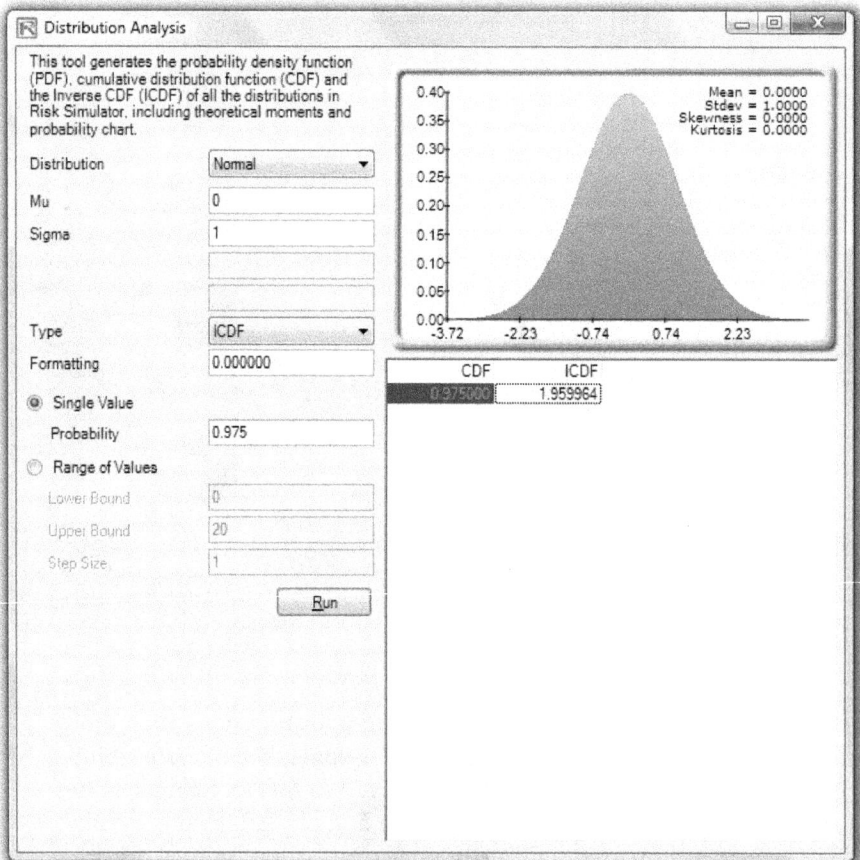

Figure 3.4: Distributional Analysis Tool (Normal ICDF and Z-score)

DISCRETE PROBABILITY DISTRIBUTIONS

To begin to understand probability distributions, consider this example: You want to look at the distribution of nonexempt wages within one department of a large company. First, you gather raw data—in this case, the wages of each nonexempt employee in the department. Second, you organize the data into a meaningful format and plot the data as a frequency distribution on a chart. To create a frequency distribution, you divide the wages into group intervals and list these intervals on the chart's horizontal axis. Then you list the number or frequency of employees in each interval on the chart's vertical axis. Now you can easily see the distribution of nonexempt wages within the department.

A glance at the chart illustrated in Figure 4.1 reveals that the employees earn from $7.00 to $9.00 per hour. You can chart this data as a probability distribution. A probability distribution shows the number of employees in each interval as a fraction of the total number of employees. To create a probability distribution, you divide the number of employees in each interval by the total number of employees and list the results on the chart's vertical axis.

Frequency Histogram

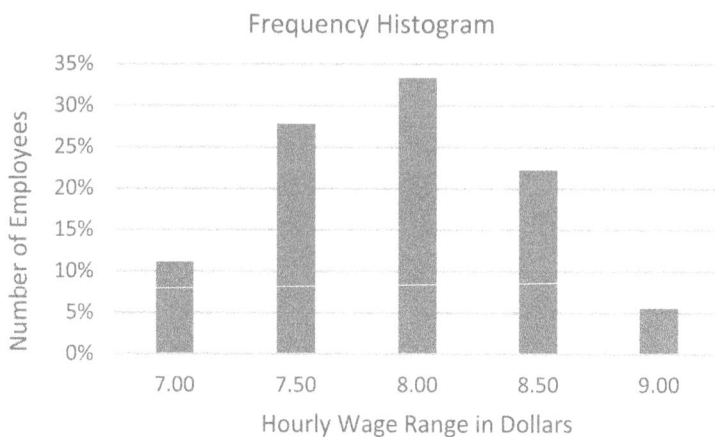

Figure 4.1: Frequency Histogram I

The chart in Figure 4.2 shows the number of employees in each wage group as a fraction of all employees; you can estimate the likelihood or probability that an employee drawn at random from the whole group earns a wage within a given interval. For example, assuming the same conditions exist at the time the sample was taken, the probability is 0.20 (a one in five chance) that an employee drawn at random from the whole group earns $8.50 an hour.

Probability distributions are either discrete or continuous. *Discrete probability distributions* describe distinct values, usually integers, with no intermediate values and are shown as a series of vertical bars. A discrete distribution, for example, might describe the number of heads in four flips of a coin as 0, 1, 2, 3, or 4. *Continuous probability distributions* are actually mathematical abstractions because they assume the existence of every possible intermediate value between two numbers; that is, a continuous distribution assumes there is an infinite number of values between any two points in the distribution. However, in many situations, you can effectively use a continuous distribution to approximate a discrete distribution even though the continuous model does not necessarily describe the situation exactly.

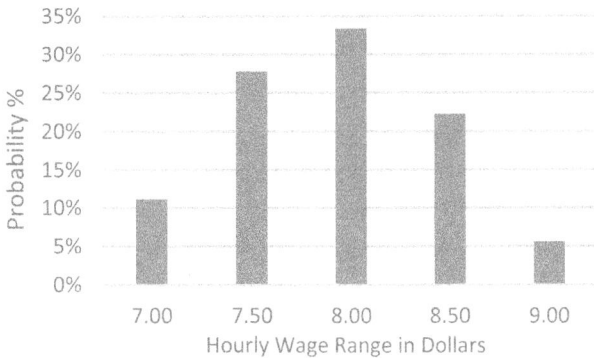

Figure 4.2: Frequency Histogram II

Selecting a Probability Distribution

Plotting data is one method for selecting a probability distribution. The following steps provide another process for selecting probability distributions that best describe the uncertain variables in your spreadsheets.

To select the correct probability distribution, use the following steps:

- Look at the variable in question. List everything you know about the conditions surrounding this variable. You might be able to gather valuable information about the uncertain variable from historical data. If historical data are not available, use your own judgment, based on experience, listing everything you know about the uncertain variable.

- Review the descriptions of the probability distributions.

- Select the distribution that characterizes this variable. A distribution characterizes a variable when the conditions of the distribution match those of the variable.

Alternatively, if you have some historical, comparable, contemporaneous, or forecast data, you can use Risk Simulator's distributional fitting modules to find the best statistical fit for your existing data. This fitting process will apply some advanced statistical techniques to find the best distribution and its relevant parameters that describe the data.

Probability Density Functions, Cumulative Distribution Functions, and Probability Mass Functions

In mathematics and Monte Carlo simulation, a probability density function (PDF) represents a *continuous* probability distribution in terms of integrals. If a probability distribution has a density of $f(x)$, then intuitively the infinitesimal interval of $[x, x + dx]$ has a probability of $f(x)\,dx$. The PDF, therefore, can be seen as a smoothed version of a probability histogram; that is, by providing an empirically large sample of a continuous random variable repeatedly, the histogram using very narrow ranges will resemble the random variable's PDF. The probability of the interval between $[a, b]$ is given by $\int_a^b f(x)dx$, which means that the total integral of the function f must be 1.0. *It is a common mistake to think of f(a) as the probability of a.* This is incorrect. In fact, $f(a)$ can sometimes be larger than 1—consider a uniform distribution between 0.0 and 0.5. The random variable x within this distribution will have $f(x)$ greater than 1. The probability, in reality, is the function $f(x)dx$ discussed above, where dx is an infinitesimal amount.

The cumulative distribution function (CDF) is denoted as $F(x) = P(X \leq x)$ indicating the probability of X taking on a less than or equal value to x. Every CDF is monotonically increasing, is continuous from the right, and at the limits has the following properties: $\lim_{x \to -\infty} F(x) = 0$ and $\lim_{x \to +\infty} F(x) = 1$. Further, the CDF is related to the PDF by $F(b) - F(a) = P(a \leq X \leq b) = \int_a^b f(x)dx$, where the PDF function f is the derivative of the CDF function F.

In probability theory, a probability mass function, or PMF, gives the probability that a *discrete* random variable is exactly equal to some value. The PMF differs from the PDF in that the values of the latter, defined only for continuous random variables, are not probabilities; rather, its integral over a set of possible values of the random variable is a probability. A random variable is discrete if its probability distribution is discrete and can be characterized by a PMF. Therefore, X is a discrete random variable if $\sum_u P(X = u) = 1$ as u runs through all possible values of the random variable X.

Therefore, a probability distribution is a listing of all possible outcomes associated with some chance process along with their associated probabilities. For example, the probability distribution of the sales of computers in a month is shown below:

Sales (x)	0	1	2	3	4	5
P(x)	0.10	0.10	0.30	0.35	0.10	0.05

From this listing, we can construct a histogram, and we could find the data's σ and μ.

Discrete probability distributions include Discrete Uniform, Binomial, Poisson, and Hypergeometric. Continuous probability distributions examples include Uniform, Normal, t, F, χ^2, etc.

BINOMIAL DISTRIBUTION

The binomial distribution describes the number of times a particular event occurs in a fixed number of trials, such as the number of heads in 10 flips of a coin or the number of defective items out of 50 items chosen.

The three conditions underlying the binomial distribution are:

- For each trial, only two outcomes are possible that are mutually exclusive.

- Trials are independent—what happens in the first trial doesn't affect the next trial.

- The probability of an event occurring remains the same from trial to trial.

The mathematical constructs for the binomial distribution are as follows:

$P(x) = \frac{n!}{x!(n-x)!} p^x (1-p)^{n-x}$ for $n > 0; x = 0, 1, 2 \dots n$; and $0 < p < 1$

$Mean = np$

$Standard\ Deviation = \sqrt{np(1-p)}$

$Skewness = \frac{1-2p}{\sqrt{np(1-p)}}$

$Excess\ Kurtosis = \frac{6p^2 - 6p + 1}{np(1-p)}$

The probability of success (p) and the integer number of total trials (n) are the distributional parameters. The number of successful trials is denoted x. It is important to note that probability of success (p) of 0 or 1 are trivial conditions and do not require any simulations, and, hence, are not allowed in the software.

Input requirements:

Probability of success > 0 and < 1 (that is, $0.0001 \leq p \leq 0.9999$)

Number of trials $\geq$ 1 or positive integers and $\leq$ 1000 (for larger trials, use the normal distribution with the relevant computed binomial mean and standard deviation as the normal distribution's parameters)

Note that the binomial distribution requires the following:

- Two outcomes in each trial—success or failure.

- Constant probability of success (p) or failure ($1 - p$).

- Statistical independence between trials.

- The probability (p) must be constant over time.

For example, if $n = 100$ toilet rolls, try calculating the $P(x = 1)$ when $= 0.5$ and $P(x = 2)$. Or consider that when $N = 10$, we are assuming a sampling without replacement, hence, the probability changes and is no longer constant. So, in a binomial distribution, we are assuming a large enough population that sampling without replacement is almost the same as sampling with replacement! In such situations, using the hypergeometric distribution is preferable.

Examples of Discrete Distribution – Binomial

Example 1: If 50% of all tissue rolls are short and you select 4 rolls at random, complete the following probabilities:

$$P(x = 0) = C_0^4(0.5)^0(0.5)^{4-0} = \frac{4!}{0!(4-0)!}(0.5)^0(0.5)^4 = \frac{1}{16} = 0.0625$$

$$P(x = 1) = C_1^4(0.5)^1(0.5)^{4-1} = \frac{4!}{1!(4-1)!}(0.5)^1(0.5)^3 = \frac{4}{16} = 0.2500$$

$$P(x = 2) = C_2^4(0.5)^2(0.5)^{4-2} = \frac{4!}{2!(4-2)!}(0.5)^2(0.5)^2 = \frac{6}{16} = 0.3750$$

$$P(x = 3) = C_3^4(0.5)^3(0.5)^{4-3} = \frac{4!}{3!(4-3)!}(0.5)^3(0.5)^1 = \frac{4}{16} = 0.2500$$

$$P(x = 4) = C_4^4(0.5)^4(0.5)^{4-4} = \frac{4!}{4!(4-4)!}(0.5)^4(0.5)^0 = \frac{1}{16} = 0.0625$$

If you draw this probability distribution, what does it look like?

This tool generates the probability density function (PDF), cumulative distribution function (CDF) and the Inverse CDF (ICDF) of all the distributions in Risk Simulator, including theoretical moments and probability chart.

Distribution: Binomial

Trials: 4

Probability: 0.5

Chart type: PDF

Type: PDF & CDF

Formatting: 0.000000

○ Single Value

Value X:

◉ Range of Values

Lower Bound: 0

Upper Bound: 4

Step Size: 1

[Run]

[Copy]

Mean = 2.0000
Stdev = 1.0000
Skewness = 0.0000
Kurtosis = -0.5000

X	PDF	CDF
0.000000	0.062500	0.062500
1.000000	0.250000	0.312500
2.000000	0.375000	0.687500
3.000000	0.250000	0.937500
4.000000	0.062500	1.000000

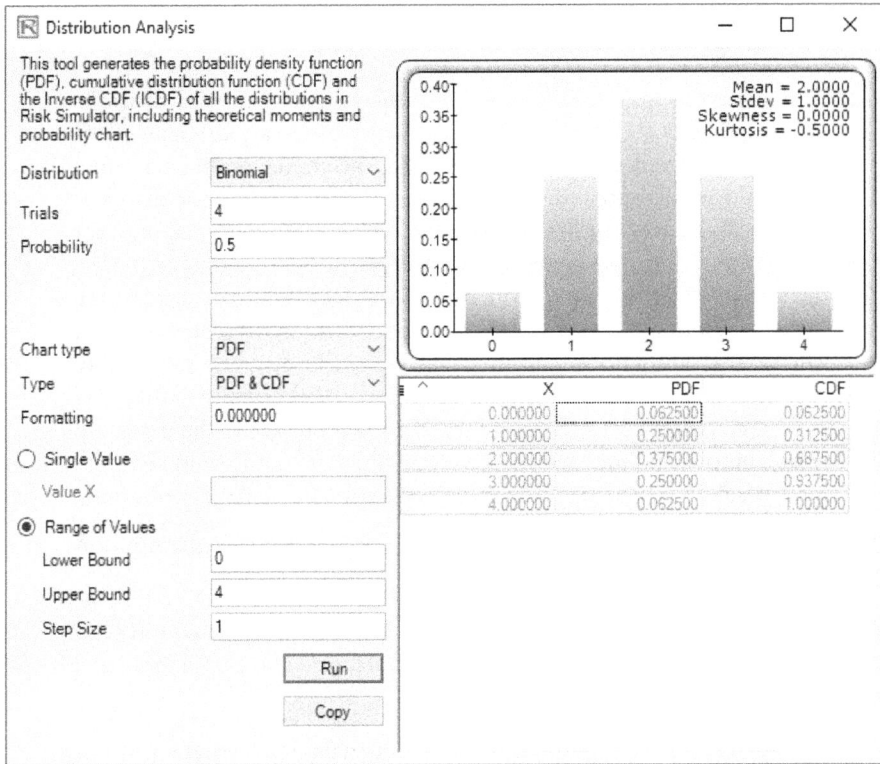

Example 2: Before modern medicine was able to detect the sex of a fetus (*chorionic villus sampling*, for the science freaks out there), psychics have long claimed to be able to predict the sex of the unborn child by looking at a picture or feeling the woman's head, and such like. This service was performed for a mere $10 fee. Oh yes, did I mention you get a money back guarantee?! So, assuming that you wish to subscribe to this service and send in a picture with a $10 check, what is the expected payoff of the swami's predictions, assuming she actually keeps her word of sending back your money should the prediction prove wrong?

$$E(x) = \Sigma x \cdot P(x) = 10\,(.5) - .32(.5) = \$4.84, \text{ including the stamp.}$$

The hypergeometric distribution is similar to the binomial distribution in that both describe the number of times a particular event occurs in a fixed number of trials. The difference is that binomial distribution trials are independent, whereas hypergeometric distribution trials change the probability for each subsequent trial and are called *trials without replacement.* For example, suppose a box of manufactured parts is known to contain some defective parts. You choose one part from the box, find it is defective, and remove the part from the box. If you choose another part from the box, the probability that it is defective is somewhat lower than for the first part because you have removed a defective part. If you had replaced the defective part, the probabilities would have remained the same, and the process would have satisfied the conditions for a binomial distribution.

The three conditions underlying the hypergeometric distribution are:

- The total number of items or elements (the population size) is a fixed number, a finite population. The population size must be less than or equal to 1,750.

- The sample size (the number of trials) represents a portion of the population.

- The known initial probability of success in the population changes after each trial.

The mathematical constructs for the hypergeometric distribution are as follows:

$$P(x) = \frac{\frac{(N_x)!}{x!(N_x-x)!} \frac{(N-N_x)!}{(n-x)!(N-N_x-n+x)!}}{\frac{N!}{n!(N-n)!}}$$

for $x = Max(n - (N - N_x), 0), ..., Min(n, N_x)$

$Mean = \frac{N_x n}{N}$

$Standard\ Deviation = \sqrt{\frac{(N-N_x)N_x n(N-n)}{N^2(N-1)}}$

$Skewness = \frac{(N-2N_x)(N-2n)}{N-2} \sqrt{\frac{N-1}{(N-N_x)N_x n(N-n)}}$

$Excess\ Kurtosis = \frac{V(N,N_x,n)}{(N-N_x)\ N_x n(-3+N)(-2+N)(-N+n)}$ where

$$V(N, N_x, n) = (N - N_x)^3 - (N - N_x)^5 + 3(N - N_x)^2 N_x - 6(N - N_x)^3 N_x$$
$$+(N - N_x)^4 N_x + 3(N - N_x) \ N_x^2 - 12(N - N_x)^2 N_x^2 + 8(N - N_x)^3 N_x^2 + N_x^3$$
$$-6(N - N_x) \ N_x^3 + 8(N - N_x)^2 N_x^3 + (N - N_x) \ N_x^4 - N_x^5 - 6(N - N_x)^3 N_x$$
$$+6(N - N_x)^4 N_x + 18(N - N_x)^2 N_x n - 6(N - N_x)^3 N_x n + 18(N - N_x) \ N_x^2 n$$
$$-24(N - N_x)^2 N_x^2 n - 6(N - N_x)^3 n - 6(N - N_x) \ N_x^3 n + 6N_x^4 n + 6(N - N_x)^2 n^2$$
$$-6(N - N_x)^3 n^2 - 24(N - N_x) \ N_x n^2 + 12(N - N_x)^2 N_x n^2 + 6N_x^2 n^2$$
$$+12(N - N_x) \ N_x^2 n^2 - 6N_x^3 n^2$$

The number of items in the population (N), trials sampled (n), and number of items in the population that have the successful trait (N_x) are the distributional parameters. The number of successful trials is denoted x.

Input requirements:

Population $\geq$ 2 and integer

Trials > 0 and integer

Successes > 0 and integer

Population > *Successes*

Trials < *Population*

Population < 1750

To reiterate, for a hypergeometric distribution:

- Dependent probabilities are acceptable.

- As n increases, the hypergeometric distribution approaches the binomial distribution.

- Use the hypergeometric distribution when $n/N \geq 0.05$, there are other statistical dependencies, or when there is a complex selection of samples from a given population.

- Sampling without replacement is assumed.

- It is a more complex combination counting rule compared to a simpler combinatorial rule in the binomial distribution.

Example: Of a group of 20 Ph.D.s in Statistics, we know that 5 of them are highly competent and the others had rich parents who donated to the school heavily and are incompetent. What is the probability that of 10 randomly selected, 3 are highly competent?

$$P(x = 3) = \frac{C_3^5 C_7^{15}}{C_{10}^{20}} = \frac{\left(\frac{5!}{3!\,(5-3)!}\right)\left(\frac{15!}{7!\,(15-7)!}\right)}{\left(\frac{20!}{10!\,(20-10)!}\right)}$$

$$= 0.348 \; or \; 34.8\%$$

POISSON DISTRIBUTION

The Poisson distribution describes the number of times an event occurs in a given interval, such as the number of telephone calls per minute or the number of errors per page in a document.

The three conditions underlying the Poisson distribution are:

- The number of possible occurrences in any interval is unlimited.

- The occurrences are independent. The number of occurrences in one interval does not affect the number of occurrences in other intervals.

- The average number of occurrences must remain the same from interval to interval.

The mathematical constructs for the Poisson are as follows:

$P(x) = \frac{e^{-\lambda}\lambda^x}{x!}$ for x and $\lambda > 0$

$Mean = \lambda$

$Standard\ Deviation = \sqrt{\lambda}$

$Skewness = \frac{1}{\sqrt{\lambda}}$

$Excess\ Kurtosis = \frac{1}{\lambda}$

Rate (λ) is the only distributional parameter.

Input requirements: $0.0001 \leq rate \leq 1000$

To reiterate, the following are the main characteristics of Poisson:

- Assumes indistinct trials.

- Models rare events where the typical probability of occurrence is small.

- When $N \geq 20$ and $\mu = np$ is ≤ 7, a Poisson is a good fit.

- Statistical independence is assumed between trials and events.

- Intervals could be subdivided into subintervals such as time and space (area).

- Assumes the probability of two or more occurrences in the same subinterval is zero.

- A good hint on when to use a Poisson distribution is when events based on time or area are measured as well as for events occurring on average.

Example: A tire service center has the capacity to service 6 customers in an hour. From prior experience, on average, 3 show up in an hour. The owner is afraid that there might be insufficient manpower to handle an overcrowding of more 6 customers. What is the probability that there will be exactly 6 customers? What about over 6 customers?

$P(x = 6) = \frac{3^6 e^{-3}}{6!} = 0.05$ and for $P(x \geq 6)$, we must add up all $P(x = 6) + P(x = 7) + P(x = 8) + \ldots$ using the Poisson table at the end of the book, we find this to be:

$1 - 0.916 = 0.084$

Examples of Hypergeometric and Poisson

$$Hypergeometric\ P(x) = \frac{C_x^k C_{n-x}^{N-k}}{C_n^N} \text{ where } \mu = n\frac{k}{N} \quad \sigma^2 = n\left(\frac{k}{N}\right)\left(1-\frac{k}{N}\right)\left(\frac{N-n}{N-1}\right)$$

$$Poisson\ P(x) = \frac{\mu^x e^{-\mu}}{x!} \text{ where } \mu = E(x) \text{ and } \sigma^2 = \mu$$

Example 1: See if you can tell which discrete distribution(s) best describes the following conditions and why (i.e., if the problem could be solved using a binomial, hypergeometric, or Poisson distribution):

(i)   A firm owns 25 trucks and each truck has a probability of 0.01 of breaking down. What is the probability of exactly 2 trucks breaking down in any given hour?

POISSON, as no distinct trials, hours could be broken up into subintervals of space and time.

(ii)   A fighter aircraft in combat has a probability of 0.01 of being shot down. What is the probability of an aircraft being shot down at least once in 15 missions?

BINOMIAL, as distinct trials and distinct success and failures, as well as statistical independence between trials.

(iii)   Four out of five dentists prefer Coolpaste to other leading toothpastes. Out of 50 dentists in the local area, if you randomly select 20 of them, what is the probability that 15 of them will prefer Coolpaste?

HYPERGEOMETRIC, as given combinations of things and given sample and population parameters, as well as sampling without replacement is assumed.

(iv)   If on average you find a mistake on 8 square yards of a rug, what is the probability that there will be a mistake on 70 yards of rug?

POISSON, as using indistinct trials, length could be broken up into an infinite number of subintervals.

(v)   Aunt Matilda's world-famous fruitcake contains on average 20 nuts per slice. If 20 mathematicians arrive and share the cake, what is the probability that each will get at least 12 nuts? What if an additional

45 Hell's Angels bikers crash the party, and she has to divide the cake for everyone?

POISSON, as using indistinct trials, area could be broken up into an infinite number of subintervals (slices).

Example 2: Calculate the respective probability for scenarios (i), (ii), and (iii) above.

- $\mu = np = 25 \times 0.01 = 0.25$ and $P(x=2)=\dfrac{(0.25)^2 \, e^{-0.25}}{2!}=0.024$

- $P(x = 1) = C_1^{15}(0.01)^1(0.99)^{14} = 0.13$

- $P(x = 15) = \dfrac{C_{15}^{40}C_5^{10}}{C_{20}^{50}} = 0.215$ as 4 out of 5 or 80% of 50 is 40

Exercises on Discrete Probability Distributions

1. A new office complex consists of 16 office suites, each of which is rented on a lease. There is a 20% chance that any one-office suite will be vacated before the lease is up.

   a. What discrete probability distribution should you be using and why?

   Binomial, as there are 2 outcomes, finite trials, fixed probabilities, discrete events, and independence.

   b. What is the probability that at least one suite will be vacated before the lease expires?

   We require $P(At\ least\ one\ vacated) = P(x = 1) + P(x = 2) + ... + P(x = 16)$, which is the same as $P(At\ least\ one\ vacated) = 1 - P(x = 0)$ since they are complementary:

   $$1 - P(x = 0) = 1 - C_x^n p^x (1 - p)^{n-x}$$
   $$= 1 - C_0^{16} 0.2^0 (1 - 0.2)^{16-0}$$

   $$= 1 - \frac{16!}{0!\,(16 - 0)!}0.2^0(0.8)^{16} = 1 - 0.0281 = 0.9719$$

c. What is the probability that no more than one suite will be vacated?

$P(No\ more\ than\ one) = P(x = 0) + P(x = 1)$ and using the binomial, we have

$$P(x = 0) + P(x = 1)$$
$$= C_0^{16} 0.2^0 (1 - 0.2)^{16-0}$$
$$+ C_1^{16} 0.2^1 (1 - 0.2)^{16-1}$$

$$= \frac{16!}{0!\,(16-0)!} 0.2^0 (0.8)^{16} + \frac{16!}{1!\,(16-1)!} 0.2^1 (0.8)^{15}$$
$$= 0.0281 + 0.1126 = 0.1407$$

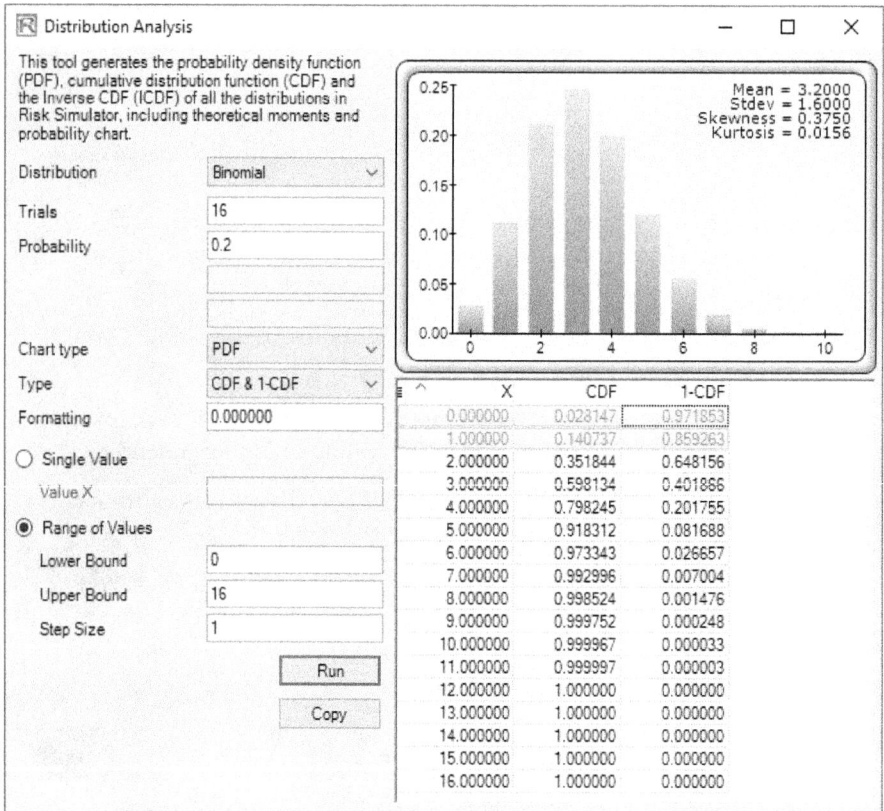

Distribution Analysis   — □ ✕

This tool generates the probability density function (PDF), cumulative distribution function (CDF) and the Inverse CDF (ICDF) of all the distributions in Risk Simulator, including theoretical moments and probability chart.

Distribution	Binomial
Trials	16
Probability	0.2
Chart type	PDF
Type	CDF & 1-CDF
Formatting	0.000000

○ Single Value
  Value X
◉ Range of Values
  Lower Bound 0
  Upper Bound 16
  Step Size 1

[Run]
[Copy]

Mean = 3.2000
Stdev = 1.6000
Skewness = 0.3750
Kurtosis = 0.0156

X	CDF	1-CDF
0.000000	0.028147	0.971853
1.000000	0.140737	0.859263
2.000000	0.351844	0.648156
3.000000	0.598134	0.401866
4.000000	0.798245	0.201755
5.000000	0.918312	0.081688
6.000000	0.973343	0.026657
7.000000	0.992996	0.007004
8.000000	0.998524	0.001476
9.000000	0.999752	0.000248
10.000000	0.999967	0.000033
11.000000	0.999997	0.000003
12.000000	1.000000	0.000000
13.000000	1.000000	0.000000
14.000000	1.000000	0.000000
15.000000	1.000000	0.000000
16.000000	1.000000	0.000000

2. In a 2016 article, *Consumer Reports* found widespread contamination and mislabeling of seafood in New York supermarkets. The study revealed that 40% of the swordfish pieces available for sale had levels of mercury above the Food and Drug Administration maximum amounts. In a random sample of 5 swordfish pieces, find the following probabilities:

    a. Four have mercury levels above the maximum levels

$$P(x = 4) = C_4^5 0.4^4 (1 - 0.4)^{5-4}$$

$$= \frac{5!}{4!\,(5 - 4)!} 0.4^4 (0.6)^1 = 0.0768$$

    b. Two have mercury levels above the maximum levels

$$P(x = 2) = C_2^5 0.4^2 (1 - 0.4)^{5-2}$$

$$= \frac{5!}{2!\,(5 - 2)!} 0.4^2 (0.6)^3 = 0.3456$$

    c. Which discrete probability distribution should you be using and why?

Binomial, since there are two outcomes, finite trials, discrete, fixed probabilities, and independence between trials.

Distribution Analysis — ☐ ✕

This tool generates the probability density function (PDF), cumulative distribution function (CDF) and the Inverse CDF (ICDF) of all the distributions in Risk Simulator, including theoretical moments and probability chart.

Distribution	Binomial
Trials	5
Probability	0.4

Chart type	PDF
Type	PDF & CDF
Formatting	0.000000

○ Single Value

Value X

◉ Range of Values

Lower Bound	0
Upper Bound	5
Step Size	1

Run

Copy

Mean = 2.0000
Stdev = 1.0954
Skewness = 0.1826
Kurtosis = -0.3667

X	PDF	CDF
0.000000	0.077760	0.077760
1.000000	0.259200	0.336960
2.000000	0.345600	0.682560
3.000000	0.230400	0.912960
4.000000	0.076800	0.989760
5.000000	0.010240	1.000000

3. A commercial for Tasteless sugarless chewing gum claims that 3 out of 4 dentists who recommend sugarless gum to their patients recommend Tasteless. Suppose this claim was established following a survey of 4 dentists randomly selected from a group of 20 dentists. What is the probability that at least 3 of the 4 dentists would recommend Tasteless if, in fact, only 50% of the original group of 20 dentists favor that brand? What discrete distribution should you use?

$P(At\ least\ 3) = P(3) + P(4)$, using the hypergeometric distribution since sampling without replacement, which creates dependence. We thus have:

$$P(3) + P(4) = \frac{C_3^{10} C_1^{10}}{C_4^{20}} + \frac{C_4^{10} C_0^{10}}{C_4^{20}} = \frac{\frac{10!}{3!\,7!} \times \frac{10!}{1!\,9!}}{\frac{20!}{4!\,16!}} + \frac{\frac{10!}{4!\,6!} \times \frac{10!}{0!\,10!}}{\frac{20!}{4!\,16!}}$$

$$= 0.2477 + 0.0433 = 0.2910$$

Distribution Analysis   — ☐ ✕

This tool generates the probability density function
(PDF), cumulative distribution function (CDF) and
the Inverse CDF (ICDF) of all the distributions in
Risk Simulator, including theoretical moments and
probability chart.

Distribution	Hypergeometric ⌄
PopulationSize	20
SampleSize	4
PopulationSuccesses	10
Chart type	PDF ⌄
Type	PDF & CDF ⌄
Formatting	0.000000

○ Single Value

   Value X

◉ Range of Values

Lower Bound	0
Upper Bound	4
Step Size	1

Run

Copy

Mean = 2.0000
Stdev = 0.9177
Skewness = 0.0000
Kurtosis = -0.3456

X	PDF	CDF
0.000000	0.043344	0.043344
1.000000	0.247678	0.291022
2.000000	0.417957	0.708978
3.000000	0.247678	0.956656
4.000000	0.043344	1.000000

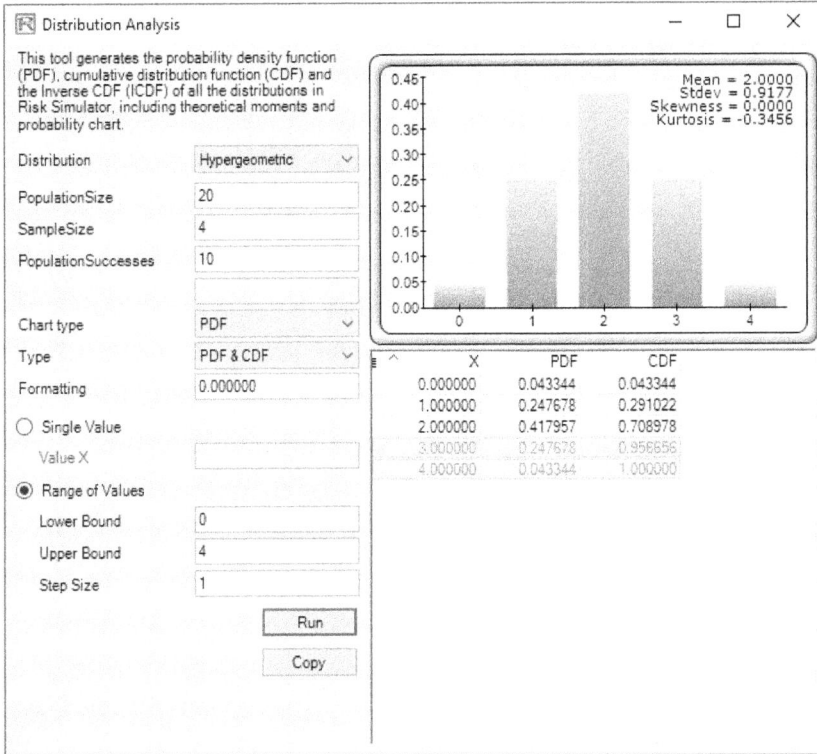

4. The Labor Management Reporting and Disclosure Act of
1959 prescribes fiduciary responsibilities for union officials
and makes embezzlement of union funds a crime. In the 38
years since the act was passed, civil suits have been filed under the law randomly and independently of one another at
an average rate of 2.7 suits per month.

   a. What is the probability that NO suits are filed in a
given month?

   Follows a Poisson distribution where

$$P(0) = \frac{\mu^x e^{-\mu}}{x!} = \frac{2.7^0 e^{-2.7}}{0!} = e^{-2.7} = 0.0672$$

   b. What is the probability of no more than 2 suits are
filed?

$$P(0) + P(1) + P(2) = \frac{2.7^0 e^{-2.7}}{0!} + \frac{2.7^1 e^{-2.7}}{1!} + \frac{2.7^2 e^{-2.7}}{2!} =$$

$$0.0672 + 0.1814 + 0.2449 = 0.4935$$

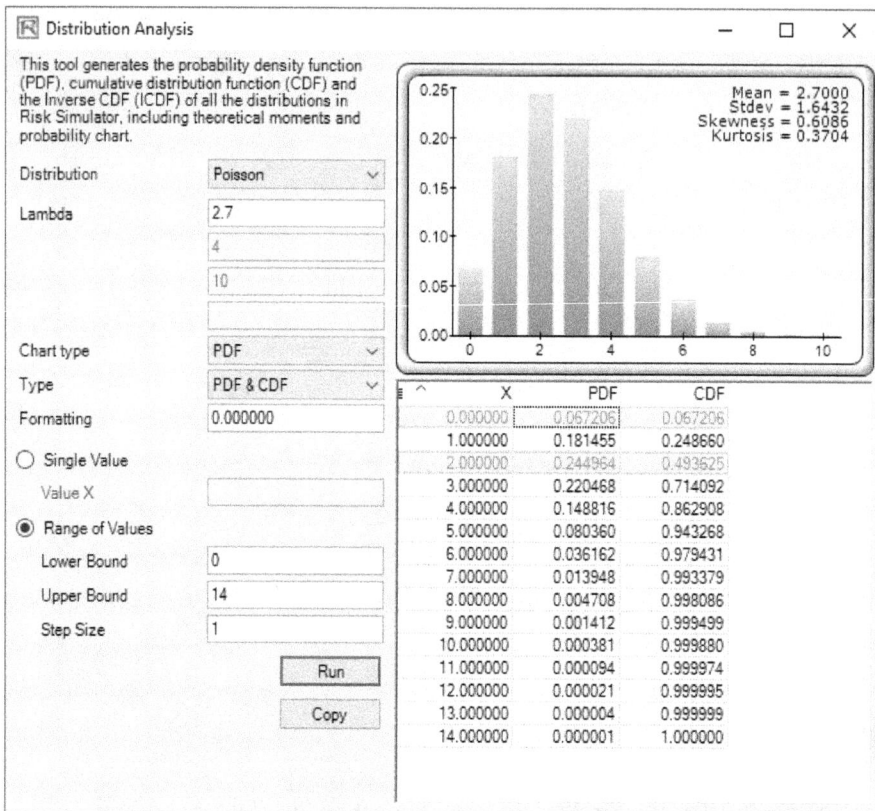

Distribution Analysis — □ ✕

This tool generates the probability density function (PDF), cumulative distribution function (CDF) and the Inverse CDF (ICDF) of all the distributions in Risk Simulator, including theoretical moments and probability chart.

Distribution	Poisson ∨
Lambda	2.7
	4
	10
Chart type	PDF ∨
Type	PDF & CDF ∨
Formatting	0.000000

○ Single Value

Value X ▢

◉ Range of Values

Lower Bound	0
Upper Bound	14
Step Size	1

[Run]

[Copy]

Mean = 2.7000
Stdev = 1.6432
Skewness = 0.6086
Kurtosis = 0.3704

X	PDF	CDF
0.000000	0.067206	0.067206
1.000000	0.181455	0.248660
2.000000	0.244964	0.493625
3.000000	0.220468	0.714092
4.000000	0.148816	0.862908
5.000000	0.080360	0.943268
6.000000	0.036162	0.979431
7.000000	0.013948	0.993379
8.000000	0.004708	0.998086
9.000000	0.001412	0.999499
10.000000	0.000381	0.999880
11.000000	0.000094	0.999974
12.000000	0.000021	0.999995
13.000000	0.000004	0.999999
14.000000	0.000001	1.000000

5. Calculate the following:

   a. $C_4^7 = \dfrac{7!}{4!(7-4)!} = \dfrac{7\times6\times5\times4\times3\times2\times1}{(4\times3\times2\times1)(3\times2\times1)} = 35$

   b. $C_6^{11} = \dfrac{11!}{6!(11-6)!} = \dfrac{11\times10\times9\times8\times7\times6\times5\times4\times3\times2\times1}{(6\times5\times4\times3\times2\times1)(5\times4\times3\times2\times1)!} = 462$

   c. $C_3^5 = \dfrac{5!}{3!(5-4)!} = \dfrac{5\times4\times3\times2\times1}{(3\times2\times1)(2\times1)!} = 10$

   d. $C_0^8 = \dfrac{8!}{0!(8-0)!} = 1$

   e. $C_8^8 = \dfrac{8!}{8!(8-8)!} = 1$

6. Suppose there are 420 applicants for 7 positions at a certain company, and the company is able to narrow the field to 22 equally qualified applicant finalists. Of the finalists, 9 are minority candidates. Assume that the 7 who are chosen are selected at random from this final group of 22. Calculate the probability that:

a. 4 of the 7 hired are minority candidates

$$P(x = 4) = \frac{C_4^9 C_3^{13}}{C_7^{22}} = \frac{\frac{9!}{4! \, 5!} \times \frac{13!}{3! \, 10!}}{\frac{22!}{7! \, 15!}} = 0.2113$$

b. None of the minority candidates is hired

$$P(x = 0) = \frac{C_0^9 C_7^{13}}{C_7^{22}} = \frac{\frac{9!}{0! \, 9!} \times \frac{13!}{7! \, 6!}}{\frac{22!}{7! \, 15!}} = 0.0101$$

c. Only 1 of those hired is a minority candidate

$$P(x = 1) = \frac{C_1^9 C_6^{13}}{C_7^{22}} = \frac{\frac{9!}{1! \, 8!} \times \frac{13!}{6! \, 7!}}{\frac{22!}{7! \, 15!}} = 0.0906$$

d. Which discrete distribution should be used here?

Hypergeometric (selection without replacement and dependence)

This tool generates the probability density function (PDF), cumulative distribution function (CDF) and the Inverse CDF (ICDF) of all the distributions in Risk Simulator, including theoretical moments and probability chart.

Distribution	Hypergeometric ⌄
PopulationSize	22
SampleSize	9
PopulationSuccesses	7
Chart type	PDF ⌄
Type	PDF & CDF ⌄
Formatting	0.0000

○ Single Value

   Value X   [ ]

◉ Range of Values

   Lower Bound   0

   Upper Bound   5

   Step Size   1

[Run]

[Copy]

Mean = 2.8636
Stdev = 1.0994
Skewness = 0.0662
Kurtosis = -0.1563

X	PDF	CDF
0.0000	0.0101	0.0101
1.0000	0.0906	0.1006
2.0000	0.2717	0.3723
3.0000	0.3522	0.7245
4.0000	0.2113	0.9358
5.0000	0.0576	0.9934

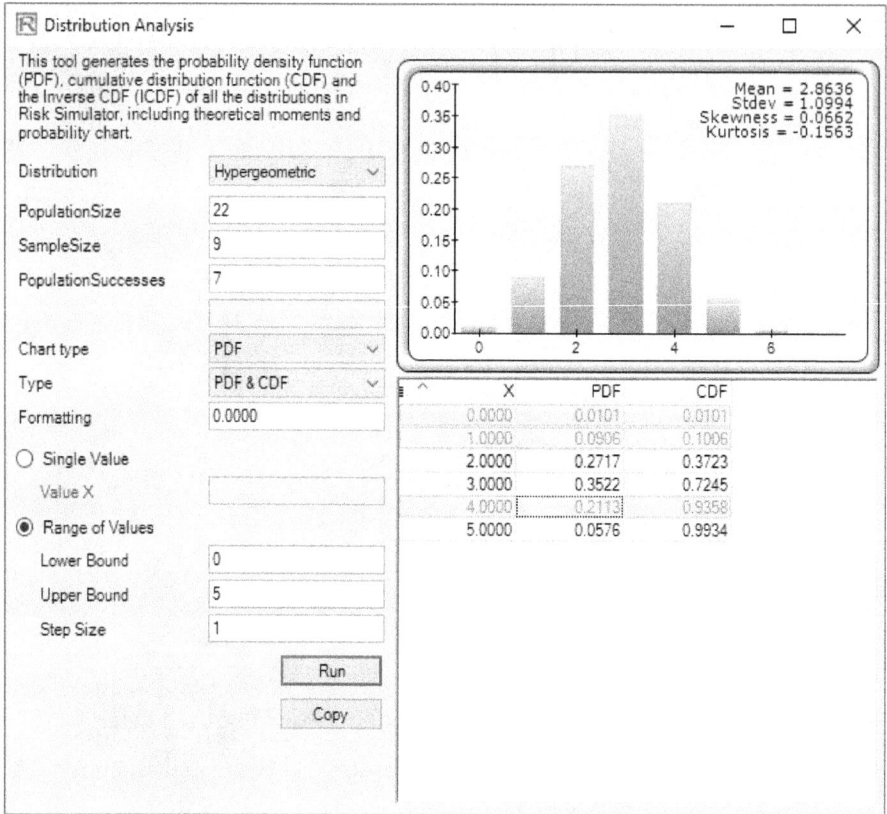

7. A sprinkler system inside an office building has two types of activation devices, A1 and A2, which operate independently. In case of fire, the probability that device A1 operates correctly is 90%, and 80% that device A2 operates correctly. If a fire breaks out, find the probability that:

   a. Both devices operate correctly

$$P(A1 \ and \ A2) = P(A1)P(A2) = (0.9)(0.8) = 0.72$$

   b. At least one device operates correctly

$$P(At \ Least \ One) = P(A1 \cap A2) \ or \ P(A1 \cap Not \ A2) \ or$$
$$P(Not \ A1 \cap A2) \ \text{is the same as}$$

$$P(At \ Least \ One) = 1 - P(Not \ A1 \cap Not \ A2)$$

$$= 1 - (1 - 0.9)(1 - 0.8) = 0.98$$

c. Exactly one device fails to operate correctly

$P(Exactly\ One)\ =\ P(A1 \cap Not\ A2)\ or\ P(Not\ A1 \cap A2)$

$P(Exactly\ One)\ =\ P(A1)\ P(Not\ A2)\ +\ P(Not\ A1)\ P(A2)$

$P(Exactly\ One)\ =\ 0.9(1-0.8)\ +\ (1-0.9)(0.8)\ =\ 0.26$

d. Neither device operates correctly

$P(Neither\ Works)\ =\ P(Not\ A1 \cap Not\ A2)$

$P(Neither\ Works)\ =\ P(Not\ A1)\ P(Not\ A2)\ =$

$(1-0.9)(1-0.8)\ =\ 0.02$

e. No more than one device operates correctly

$P(No\ More\ Than\ One)\ =\ 1-P(A1 \cap A2)$

$P(No\ More\ Than\ One)\ =\ 1-P(A1)P(A2)$

$=\ 1-0.9(0.8)\ =\ 0.28$

APPENDIX—ADDITIONAL DISCRETE DISTRIBUTIONS

Following are several additional discrete distributions complete with a detailed listing of their properties. This listing is included in the current appendix for the reader's reference.

Bernoulli or Yes/No Distribution

The Bernoulli distribution is a discrete distribution with two outcomes (e.g., heads or tails, success or failure, 0 or 1). The Bernoulli distribution is the binomial distribution with one trial and can be used to simulate Yes/No or Success/Failure conditions. This distribution is the fundamental building block of other more complex distributions. For instance:

- Binomial distribution: Bernoulli distribution with higher number of n total trials and computes the probability of x successes within this total number of trials.

- Geometric distribution: Bernoulli distribution with higher number of trials and computes the number of failures required before the first success occurs.

- Negative binomial distribution: Bernoulli distribution with higher number of trials and computes the number of failures before the xth success occurs.

The mathematical constructs for the Bernoulli distribution are:

$$P(x) = \begin{cases} 1-p & \text{for } x = 0 \\ p & \text{for } x = 1 \end{cases}$$

$$P(x) = p^x(1-p)^{1-x}$$

$$Mean = p$$

$$Standard\ Deviation = \sqrt{p(1-p)}$$

$$Skewness = \frac{1-2p}{\sqrt{p(1-p)}}$$

$$Excess\ Kurtosis = \frac{6p^2 - 6p + 1}{p(1-p)}$$

The probability of success (p) is the only distributional parameter. Also, it is important to note that there is only one trial in the Bernoulli distribution, and the resulting simulated value is 0 or 1.

Input requirements: $0 < $ *Probability of success* $ < 1$ (that is, $0.0001 \leq p \leq 0.9999$)

Discrete Uniform Distribution

The discrete uniform distribution is also known as the *equally likely outcomes* distribution, where the distribution has a set of N elements, and each element has the same probability. This distribution is related to the uniform distribution, but its elements are discrete and not continuous. The mathematical constructs for the discrete uniform distribution are:

$$P(x) = \frac{1}{N}$$

$Mean = \frac{N+1}{2}$ ranked value

$Standard\ Deviation = \sqrt{\frac{(N-1)(N+1)}{12}}$ ranked value

$Skewness = 0$ (that is, the distribution is perfectly symmetrical)

$Excess\ Kurtosis = \frac{-6(N^2+1)}{5(N-1)(N+1)}$ ranked value

Input requirements: *Minimum* $<$ *Maximum* and both must be integers (negative integers and zero are allowed)

Geometric Distribution

The geometric distribution describes the number of trials until the first successful occurrence, such as the number of times you need to spin a roulette wheel before you win.

The three conditions underlying the geometric distribution are:

- The number of trials is not fixed.

- The trials continue until the first success.

- The probability of success is the same from trial to trial.

The mathematical constructs for the geometric distribution are:

$$P(x) = p(1-p)^{x-1} \quad \text{for } 0 < p < 1 \text{ and } x = 1, 2, \ldots, n$$

$$Mean = \frac{1}{p} - 1$$

$$Standard\ Deviation = \sqrt{\frac{1-p}{p^2}}$$

$$Skewness = \frac{2-p}{\sqrt{1-p}}$$

$$Excess\ Kurtosis = \frac{p^2 - 6p + 6}{1-p}$$

The probability of success (p) is the only distributional parameter. The number of successful trials simulated is denoted x, which can only take on positive integers.

Input requirements: $0 <$ *Probability of success* < 1 (that is, $0.0001 \leq p \leq 0.9999$). It is important to note that probability of success (p) of 0 or 1 are trivial conditions and do not require any simulations, and, hence, are not allowed in the software.

Negative Binomial Distribution

The negative binomial distribution is useful for modeling the distribution of the number of trials until the rth successful occurrence, such as the number of sales calls you need to make to close a total of 10 orders. It is essentially a *superdistribution* of the geometric distribution. This distribution shows the probabilities of each number of trials in excess of r to produce the required success r.

The conditions underlying the negative binomial distribution are:

- The number of trials is not fixed.

- The trials continue until the rth success.

- The probability of success is the same from trial to trial.

The mathematical constructs for the negative binomial distribution are as follows:

$$P(x) = \frac{(x+r-1)!}{(r-1)!\,x!} p^r (1-p)^x \quad for\ x = r, r+1, ...;\ and\ 0 < p < 1$$

$$Mean = \frac{r(1-p)}{p}$$

$$Standard\ Deviation = \sqrt{\frac{r(1-p)}{p^2}}$$

$$Skewness = \frac{2-p}{\sqrt{r(1-p)}}$$

$$Excess\ Kurtosis = \frac{p^2 - 6p + 6}{r(1-p)}$$

Probability of success (p) and required successes (r) are the distributional parameters.

Input requirements:

$0 < Successes\ required\ must\ be\ positive\ integers < 8000$

$0.0001 < Probability\ of\ success < 0.9999$

It is important to note that probability of success (p) of 0 or 1 are trivial conditions and do not require any simulations, and, hence, are not allowed in the software.

Pascal Distribution

The Pascal distribution is useful for modeling the distribution of the number of total trials needed to obtain the number of successful occurrences required. For instance, to close a total of 10 sales opportunities, how many total sales calls would you need to make given some probability of success in each call? Imagine a chart with its x-axis showing the total number of calls required, which includes successful and failed calls. The number of trials is not fixed, the trials continue until the Rth success, and the probability of success is the same from trial to trial. Pascal distribution is related to the negative binomial distribution. Negative binomial distribution computes the number of events needed in addition to the number of successes required given some probability (in other words, the total failures), whereas the Pascal distribution computes the total number of events needed (in other words, the sum of failures and successes) to achieve the successes required given some probability. Probability and Successes Required are the two distributional parameters.

The mathematical constructs for the Pascal distribution are:

$$f(x) = \begin{cases} \frac{(x-1)!}{(x-s)!(s-1)!}p^S(1-p)^{X-S} \text{ for all } x \geq s \\ 0 \text{ otherwise} \end{cases}$$

$$F(x) = \begin{cases} \sum_{x=1}^{k} \frac{(x-1)!}{(x-s)!(s-1)!}p^S(1-p)^{X-S} \text{ for all } x \geq s \\ 0 \text{ otherwise} \end{cases}$$

$$Mean = \frac{s}{p}$$

$$Standard\ Deviation = \sqrt{s(1-p)p^2}$$

$$Skewness = \frac{2-p}{\sqrt{r(1-p)}}$$

$$Excess\ Kurtosis = \frac{p^2-6p+6}{r(1-p)}$$

The conditions underlying the Pascal as well as the negative binomial distribution are:

- The number of trials is not fixed.

- The trials continue until the Rth success.

- The probability of success is the same from trial to trial.

Successes Required and Probability are the distributional parameters.

Input requirements:

$Successes\ required\ > 0$ and is an integer

$0 \leq Probability \leq 1$

CONTINUOUS PROBABILITY DISTRIBUTIONS

With discrete distributions, we use the probability mass function (PMF), where we simply add the exact probabilities to obtain the cumulative probability distribution (CDF). In a continuous probability distribution, we use the continuous counterpart, which is the probability density function (PDF). Integration calculus is required to obtain a continuous distribution's CDF.

In a discrete PMF, the probability of x is a particular value, but the exact probability in a continuous distribution is equal to 0. So, we usually use a range of values when dealing with continuous distributions. This chapter looks at using the standard normal distribution and presents the concept of confidence intervals. Standard normal simply means using a standard set of inputs for the normal distribution, typically with a mean of zero and a standard deviation of one, denoted as $N(0,1)$. Standardizing the data makes the math simpler to handle, and we can use a standard Z-score model, where $Z = \frac{x-\mu}{\sigma}$ so that it is not necessary to integrate every time; rather, a predetermined table can be used.

In addition, normal distributions are also used to approximate the binomial distribution as well as a variety of other distributions. See the appendix at the end of this chapter for more technical details on how various distributions are related to each other.

Examples Application of Continuous Probability Distributions

$Z = \frac{x-\mu}{\sigma}$ and use the Z table at the end of this book

Example 1: The batteries from a particular watch battery manufacturer last, on average, for 15 months with a standard deviation of 1.5 years. Assume that the battery life is normally distributed. If a battery is randomly selected from the manufacturer's production line, find the probability that it has a life of:

(i) $P(x = 15\,months) = 0$ since for a point, the probability is 0.

(ii) $P(x \geq 15\,months) = 0.50$ as half of the curve or $Z = (15 - 15)/1.5$ yields the value $Z = 0$ or an area of 0.0, hence, $0.5 - 0.0 = 0.5$.

(iii) $P(x \geq 16.5\,months) \Rightarrow Z = (16.5 - 15)/1.5 = 1$ or $A = 0.3413$. Hence, we have $0.5 - 0.3413 = 0.1587 = 15.87\%$. See the diagram below.

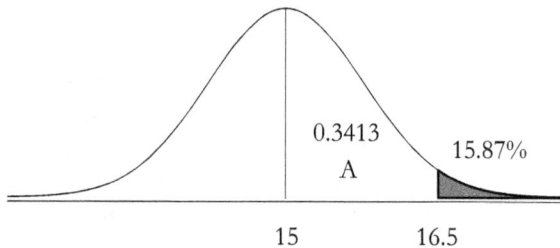

A Z-value of 1 on a Normal (0,1) can be obtained using Risk Simulator's Distributional Analysis Tool as shown on the left in the accompanying figure. The CDF is the left tail and the *1 – CDF* value is the right tail. For the problem above, the right tail is required, which yields 15.87%.

Alternatively, use Excel and enter the function "*=NORMSDIST(1)*", which will return the CDF of 84.13% for the left tail, or "*=1–NORMSDIST(1)*", which will return 15.87% for the right tail.

An even simpler approach may be to use Risk Simulator's Distributional Analysis Tool to enter the mean of 15 and standard deviation of 1.5 into a normal distribution and compute the CDF of 16.5 months (see below, right figure). The tool returns the *1 – CDF* or right tail of 15.87%.

The tool makes the computations directly without the need to obtain the Z-scores and convert them into probabilities.

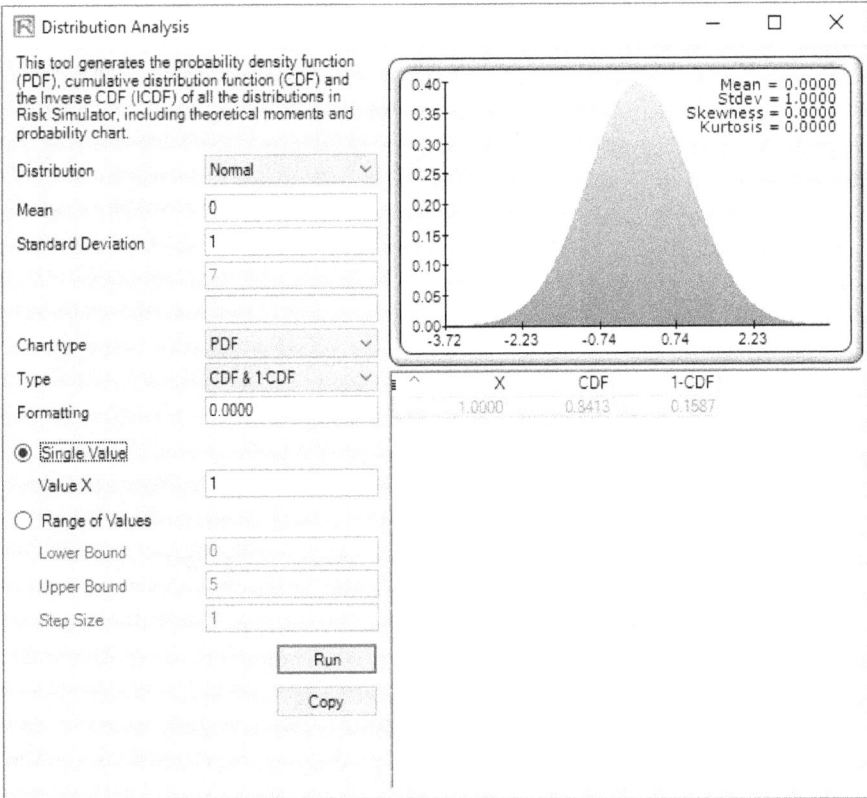

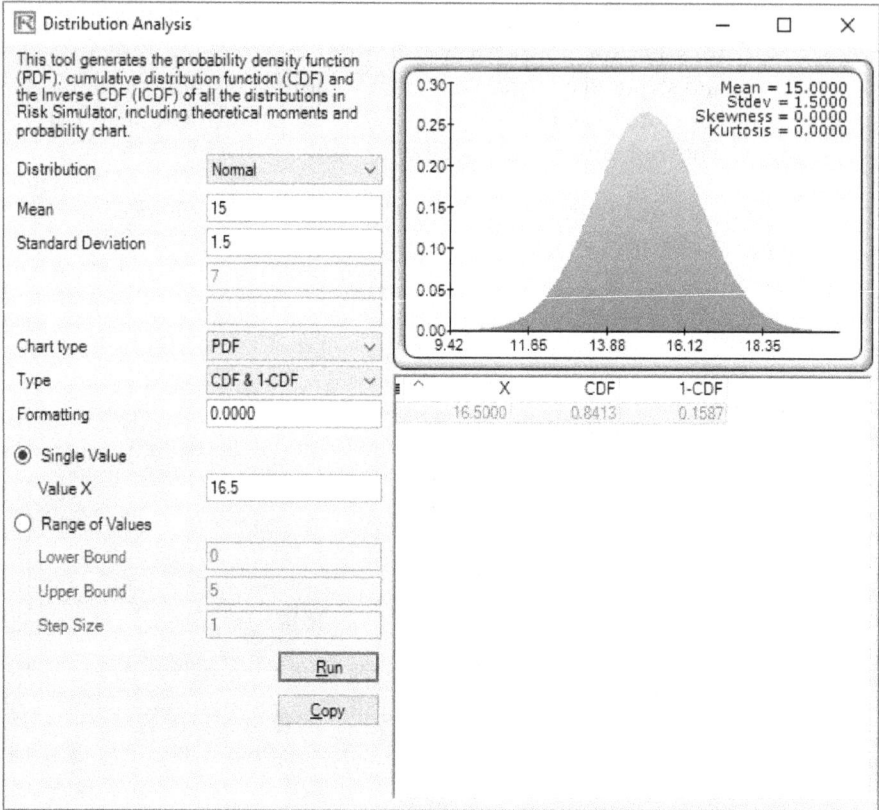

Distribution Analysis — □ ✕

This tool generates the probability density function (PDF), cumulative distribution function (CDF) and the Inverse CDF (ICDF) of all the distributions in Risk Simulator, including theoretical moments and probability chart.

Distribution	Normal
Mean	15
Standard Deviation	1.5
	7
Chart type	PDF
Type	CDF & 1-CDF
Formatting	0.0000

◉ Single Value

| Value X | 16.5 |

○ Range of Values

Lower Bound	0
Upper Bound	5
Step Size	1

Run

Copy

Mean = 15.0000
Stdev = 1.5000
Skewness = 0.0000
Kurtosis = 0.0000

Chart x-axis: 9.42 11.65 13.88 16.12 18.35

X	CDF	1-CDF
16.5000	0.8413	0.1587

Example 2: The battery manufacturer from example 1 wants to offer a 12-month warranty on her batteries: a full refund if the battery dies before 12 months. What are the chances that this refund will have to be provided?

So, we get $P(x \leq 12) \Rightarrow Z = (12 - 15)/1.5 = -2.0$ or $A = 0.4772$ to the left since a negative Z. Hence, $0.5 - 0.4772 = 0.0228$ or 2.28% probability.

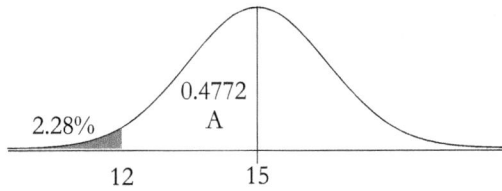

Using a Z score of –2.0, we get 2.28% using Risk Simulator (below, left) and in Excel, "=NORMSDIST(-2)" yields 2.28%. Alternatively, direct calculations using a normal distribution's CDF also yields 2.28% (below, right).

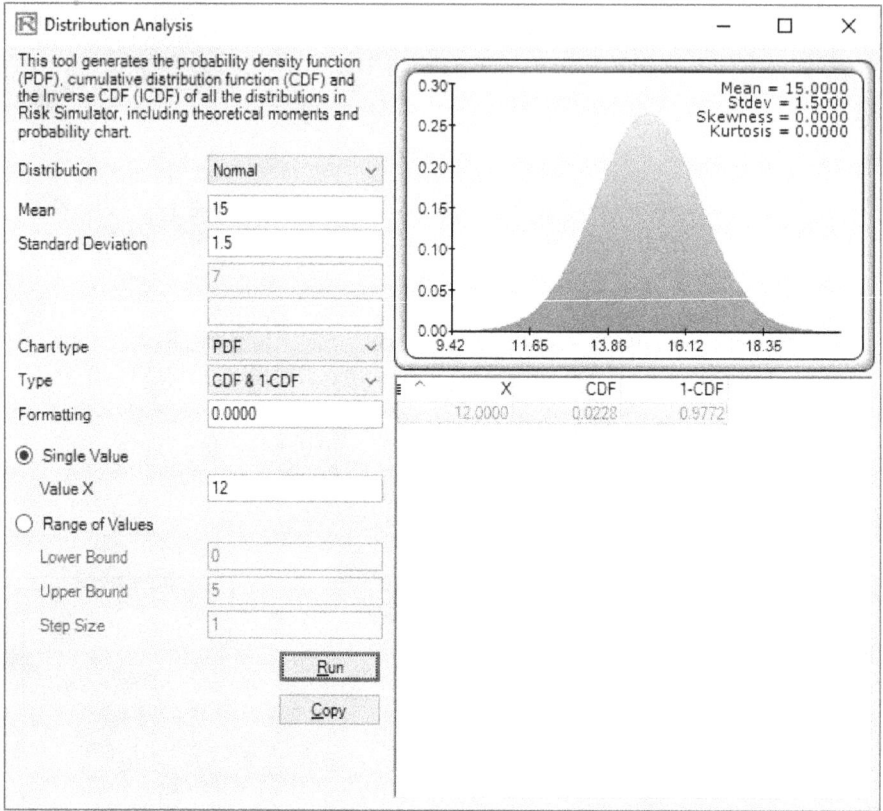

Distribution Analysis — □ X

This tool generates the probability density function (PDF), cumulative distribution function (CDF) and the Inverse CDF (ICDF) of all the distributions in Risk Simulator, including theoretical moments and probability chart.

Distribution	Normal
Mean	15
Standard Deviation	1.5
	7
Chart type	PDF
Type	CDF & 1-CDF
Formatting	0.0000

◉ Single Value

Value X	12

○ Range of Values

Lower Bound	0
Upper Bound	5
Step Size	1

Run

Copy

Mean = 15.0000
Stdev = 1.5000
Skewness = 0.0000
Kurtosis = 0.0000

Chart x-axis: 9.42 11.65 13.88 16.12 18.35

X	CDF	1-CDF
12.0000	0.0228	0.9772

Example 3: Suppose the probability calculated in example 2 is too high and, hence, too costly for the manufacturer. To minimize the cost and lower the probability of having to make a refund to a 1% probability, what would be a suitable warranty date (in months)?

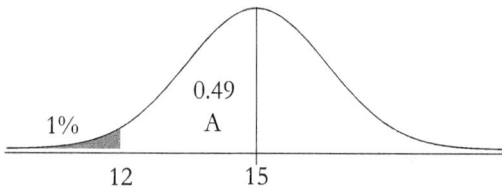

Working backwards, to obtain a $P(x \leq X) = 0.01$, first look at the graph and then find the Z value for $A = 0.49$, which yields $Z = 2.33$. Hence, $Z = -2.33 = (x - 15)/1.5$. Solving, $x = (-2.33 \times 1.5) + 15 = 11.5$ months. Watch out! If you use 2.33 without the negative sign, you get 18 months, which does not make any sense! Similarly, you can easily solve the problem by using Risk Simulator to compute the Inverse CDF (ICDF) on a 1% CDF left-tail probability, which yields 11.5 months (see the next figure).

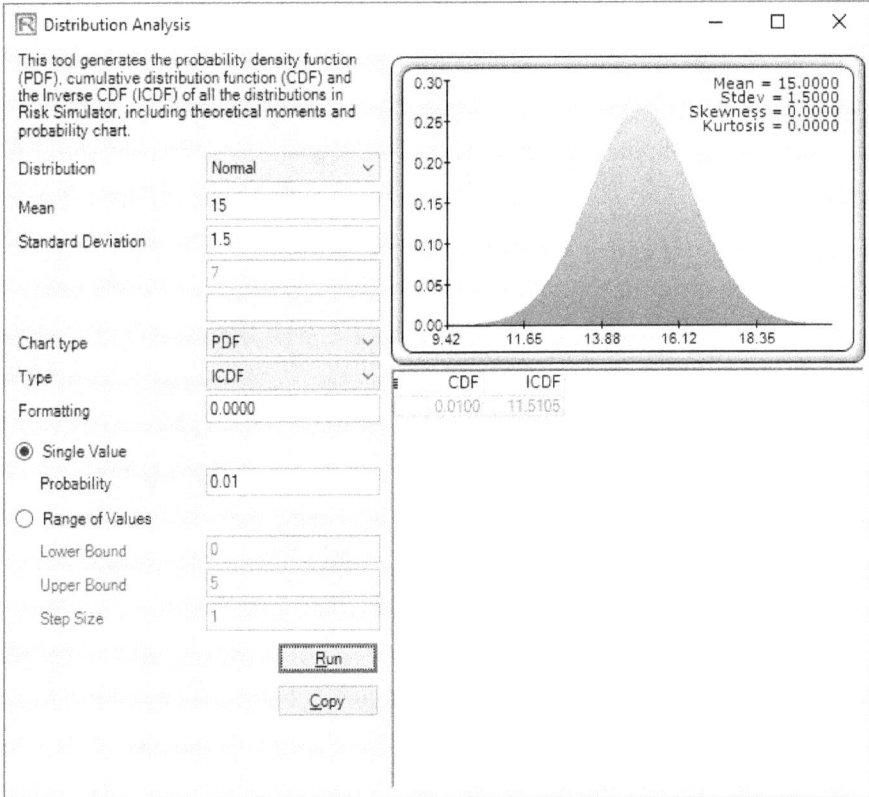

Example 4: The population mean of an IQ test based on the Cattel scale is 100, and its standard deviation is 15; the *genius threshold* is 140 points while the *not so genius threshold* is 50. What is the probability that an individual is a genius? What is the probability that an individual is below this threshold?

(i)   For $P(x \geq 140) \Rightarrow Z = (140 - 100)/15 = 2.67, A = 0.4926$. Hence, $0.5 - 0.4962 = 0.0038$ or 0.38% or about 4 people in 1,000 would be considered a genius.

(ii) $P(x \le 50) \Rightarrow Z = (50 - 100)/15 = -3.33$ yielding
$A = 0.4996$, the probability of being not so smart is
$0.5 - 0.4996 = 0.0004$ or 0.04%.

Examples of Continuous Distributions, Point and Interval Estimates

Example 1: Use the table of standard normal probability distribution at the end of this book to determine the following. To facilitate answering the question, draw a standard normal curve and shade in the area you are attempting to calculate.

(i) $P(0.00 < z < 1.96) = 47.5\%$

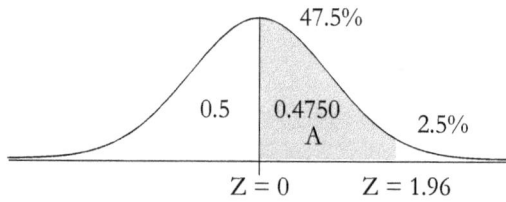

47.5%

0.5   0.4750
       A

2.5%

Z = 0   Z = 1.96

(ii) $P(z > 1.64) = 1 - (0.5 + 0.4495) = 5\%$

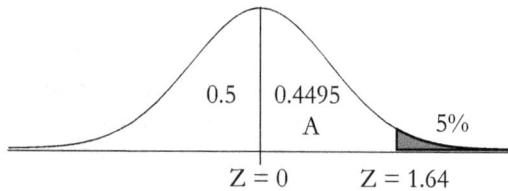

0.5   0.4495
       A

5%

Z = 0   Z = 1.64

(iii) $P(z < 1.28) = 0.5 + 0.3997 = 89.97\%$

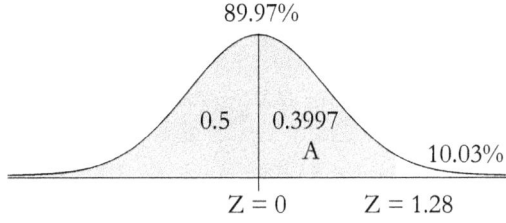

89.97%

0.5   0.3997

A

10.03%

$Z = 0$ $Z = 1.28$

(iv) $P(-2.00 < z < 2.00) = 0.4772 + 0.4772 = 95.44\%$

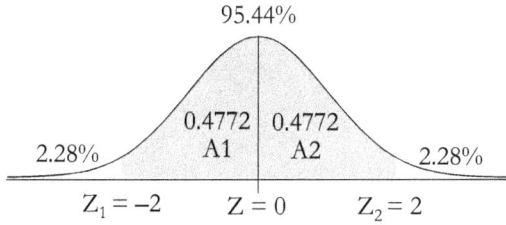

95.44%

0.4772   0.4772

2.28%   A1   A2   2.28%

$Z_1 = -2$ $Z = 0$ $Z_2 = 2$

(v) $P(z < 1.50) = 0.4332 + 0.5 = 93.32\%$

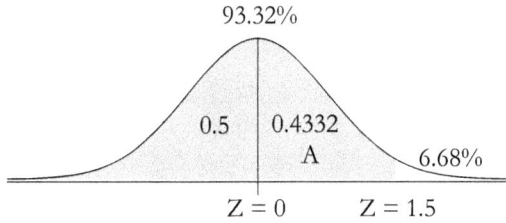

93.32%

0.5   0.4332

A

6.68%

$Z = 0$ $Z = 1.5$

Example 2: A psychology study finds that the distribution of college students' ages in a certain city follows a normal distribution. The average was found to be 20.0 with a standard deviation of 4.0 for the population.

(i)   Find the probability that student randomly chosen has an age exceeding 23.

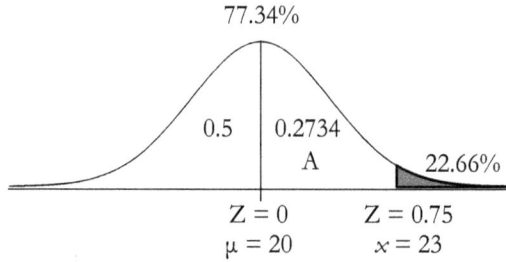

77.34%

0.5 | 0.2734
A
22.66%

Z = 0   Z = 0.75
μ = 20   x = 23

$Z = \frac{23-20}{4} = 0.75$ and

$P(x \geq 23) = 1 - (0.5 + 0.2734) = 22.66\%$

(ii)   What proportion of all values are less than 22?

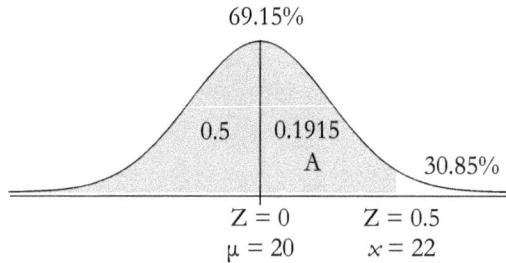

69.15%

0.5 | 0.1915
A
30.85%

Z = 0   Z = 0.5
μ = 20   x = 22

$Z = \frac{22-20}{4} = 0.5$ and

$P(x \leq 22) = 0.1915 + 0.5 = 69.15\%$

(iii)   What is the probability of a value lying between 19 and 22?

29.02%

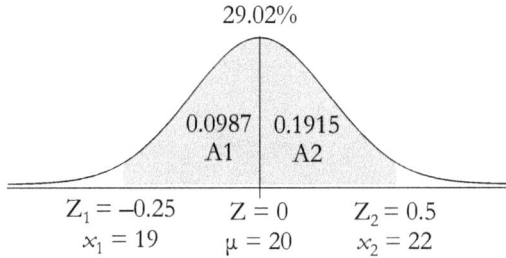

$Z_1 = -0.25$ $Z = 0$ $Z_2 = 0.5$
$x_1 = 19$ $\mu = 20$ $x_2 = 22$

$Z_1 = \frac{19-20}{4} = -0.25$ and $Z_2 = \frac{22-20}{4} = 0.50$

we have $P(19 \leq x \leq 22) = 0.0987 + 0.1915 = 29.02\%$

(iv)   Find the age corresponding to a Z value of 1.88.

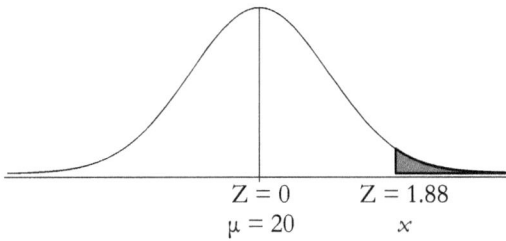

$Z = 0$ $Z = 1.88$
$\mu = 20$ x

$Z = \frac{X-20}{4} = 1.88$ we have $x = 4(1.88) + 20 = 27.52$

(v)   Find the age corresponding to a z value of –2.33.

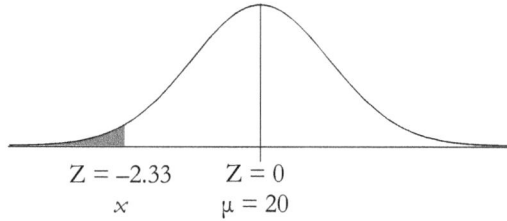

Z = –2.33   Z = 0
    x   μ = 20

$Z = \frac{X-20}{4} = -2.33$ we have

$x = 4(-2.33) + 20 = 10.68$

(vi)   What value is greater than 60% of all values?

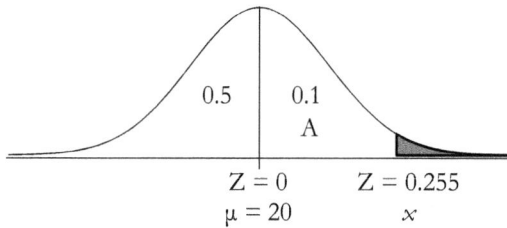

0.5 | 0.1
        A

Z = 0   Z = 0.255
μ = 20   x

A = 0.10 gets Z = 0.255

$Z = \frac{X-20}{4} = 0.255$ and we have

$x = 4(0.255) + 20 = 21.02$

Example 3: The operating life of 50-gallon hot water heaters is known to be normally distributed with a mean of 12 years and a standard deviation of 3 years. The heaters are all sold with an 8-year guarantee. Sketch a normal distribution and shade the appropriate areas.

(i)   What proportion of customers will get double the guaranteed life, that is, an operating life of 16 years?

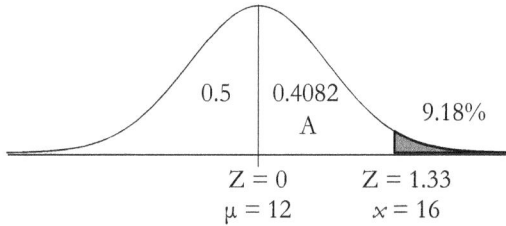

$Z_{16} = \frac{16-12}{3} = 1.33$ yielding $A = 0.4082$

while $P(x \geq 16) = 1 - (0.5 + 0.4082) = 9.18\%$

(ii)   What proportion of heaters will be eligible to be returned for failing to satisfy the guarantee?

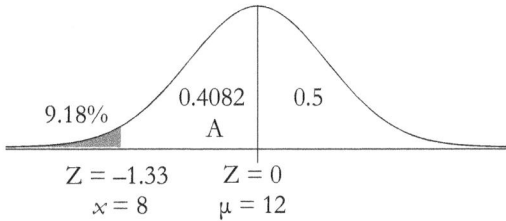

$Z_8 = \frac{8-12}{3} = -1.33$ yielding $A = 0.4082$

while $P(x \leq 8) = 0.5 - 0.4082 = 9.18\%$

Example 4: The wages of mechanics working for a small airline are known to be normally distributed with a mean of $35,000 and a standard deviation of $5,000.

(i)   What proportion of mechanics received a wage greater than $50,000?

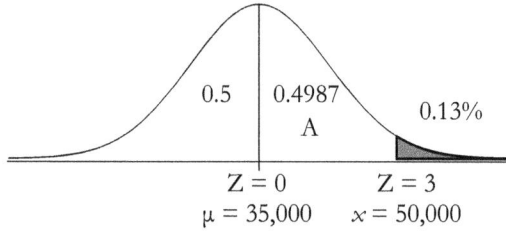

$$Z_{50000} = \frac{50000-35000}{5000} = 3.0 \text{ yielding } A = 0.4987$$

while $P(x \geq 50000) = 0.5 - 0.4987 = 0.13\%$

(ii)   What is the probability that a mechanic's wage is less than $30,000?

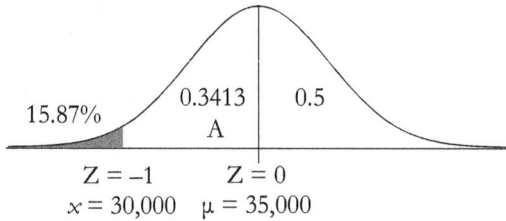

$$Z_{30000} = \frac{30000-35000}{5000} = -1.0 \text{ yielding } A = 0.3413$$

while $P(x \leq 30000) = 1 - (0.5 + 0.3413) = 15.87\%$

(iii)   What is the third quartile of the wages for the mechanics?

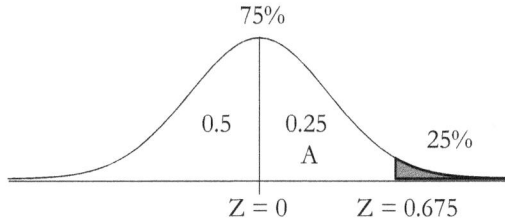

$$A = 0.25 \text{ yields } Z = 0.675 = \frac{X - 35000}{5000}$$

and $x = 5000(0.675) + 35000 = \$38{,}375$

Example 5: Calculate the 95% confidence interval for a population mean for each condition:

(i) $\bar{x} = 680 \; \sigma = 20 \; n = 70$

$680 \pm 1.96 \frac{20}{\sqrt{70}}$ means a confidence range of

675.315 to 684.685

(ii) $\bar{x} = 31 \; \sigma = 9 \; n = 50$

$31 \pm 1.96 \frac{9}{\sqrt{50}}$ means a confidence range of

28.505 to 33.495

(iii) $\bar{x} = 26{,}000 \; \sigma = 48{,}000 \; n = 500$

$26000 \pm 1.96 \frac{48000}{\sqrt{500}}$ means a confidence range of

21792 to 30207

Example 6: The following amounts from telephone bills for 10 residential homes in a particular town have historically been found to follow a normal distribution:

$20.95	$123.50	$55.00	$38.95
$75.00	$155.00	$23.50	$79.90
$50.50	$100.50		

(i)   Estimate the monthly telephone bill for the town using a point estimate and calculate the 95% confidence interval.

Calculated $\bar{x} = 72.28$ and $s = 43.7493$

$$72.28 \pm 1.96 \frac{43.7493}{\sqrt{10}}$$

means a confidence range of 45.1639 to 99.3961

(ii)   How large a sample of residential homes' telephone bills would have to be taken to make the error of estimate no more than $5.00?

$$5 = 1.96 \frac{43.7493}{\sqrt{n}} \text{ means } n = \frac{1.96^2(43.7493)^2}{5^2} = 294$$

Following is a detailed listing of the different types of continuous probability distributions that can be used in Monte Carlo simulation.

Arcsine Distribution

The arcsine distribution is U-shaped and is a special case of the beta distribution when both shape and scale are equal to 0.5. Values close to the minimum and maximum have high probabilities of occurrence whereas values between these two extremes have very small probabilities of occurrence. Minimum and maximum are the distributional parameters.

The mathematical constructs for the arcsine distribution are shown below. The probability density function (PDF) is denoted $f(x)$ and the cumulative distribution function (CDF) is denoted $F(x)$.

$$f(x) = \begin{cases} \frac{1}{\pi\sqrt{x(1-x)}} & for\ 0 \leq x \leq 1 \\ 0 & otherwise \end{cases}$$

$$F(x) = \begin{cases} 0 & x < 0 \\ \frac{2}{\pi} sin^{-1}(\sqrt{x}) & 0 \leq x \leq 1 \\ 1 & x > 1 \end{cases}$$

$$Mean = \frac{Min+Max}{2}$$

$$Standard\ Deviation = \sqrt{\frac{(Max-Min)^2}{8}}$$

$$Skewness = 0\ for\ all\ inputs$$

$$Excess\ Kurtosis = 1.5\ for\ all\ inputs$$

Minimum and maximum are the distributional parameters.

Input requirements: $Max > Min$ (either input can be positive, negative, or zero)

Beta Distribution

The beta distribution is very flexible and is commonly used to represent variability over a fixed range. One of the more important applications of the beta distribution is its use as a conjugate distribution for the parameter of a Bernoulli distribution. In this application, the beta distribution is used to represent the uncertainty in the probability of occurrence of an event. It is also used to describe empirical data and predict the random behavior of percentages and fractions, as the range of outcomes is typically between 0 and 1.

The value of the beta distribution lies in the wide variety of shapes it can assume when you vary the two parameters, alpha and beta. If the parameters are equal, the distribution is symmetrical. If either parameter is 1 and the other parameter is greater than 1, the distribution is J-shaped. If alpha is less than beta, the distribution is said to be positively skewed (most of the values are near the minimum value). If alpha is greater than beta, the distribution is negatively skewed (most of the values are near the maximum value).

The mathematical constructs for the beta distribution follow:

$$f(x) = \frac{(x)^{(\alpha-1)}(1-x)^{(\beta-1)}}{\left[\frac{\Gamma(\alpha)\Gamma(\beta)}{\Gamma(\alpha+\beta)}\right]} \quad \text{for } \alpha > 0; \beta > 0; x > 0$$

$$Mean = \frac{\alpha}{\alpha+\beta}$$

$$Standard\ Deviation = \sqrt{\frac{\alpha\beta}{(\alpha+\beta)^2(1+\alpha+\beta)}}$$

$$Skewness = \frac{2(\beta-\alpha)\sqrt{1+\alpha+\beta}}{(2+\alpha+\beta)\sqrt{\alpha\beta}}$$

$$Excess\ Kurtosis = \frac{3(\alpha+\beta+1)[\alpha\beta(\alpha+\beta-6)+2(\alpha+\beta)^2]}{\alpha\beta(\alpha+\beta+2)(\alpha+\beta+3)} - 3$$

Alpha (α) and beta (β) are the two distributional shape parameters, and Γ is the gamma function. The two conditions underlying the beta distribution are:

- The uncertain variable is a random value between 0 and a positive value.

- The distribution's shape is specified using two positive values.

Input requirements: Alpha and beta > 0 and can be any positive value

Beta 3 and Beta 4 Distributions

The original beta distribution only takes two inputs, alpha and beta shape parameters. However, the output of the simulated value is between 0 and 1. In the beta 3 distribution, we add an extra parameter called location or shift, where we are not free to move away from this 0 to 1 output limitation, therefore the beta 3 distribution is also known as a shifted beta distribution. Similarly, the beta 4 distribution adds two input parameters, location, or shift, and factor. The original beta distribution is multiplied by the factor and shifted by the location, and therefore the beta 4 is also known as the multiplicative shifted beta distribution.

The mathematical constructs for the beta 3 and beta 4 distributions are based on those in the beta distribution, with the relevant shifts and factorial multiplication (e.g., the PDF and CDF will be adjusted by the shift and factor, and some of the moments, such as the mean, will similarly be affected; the standard deviation, in contrast, is only affected by the factorial multiplication, whereas the remaining moments are not affected at all).

Input requirements: Location can take on any positive or negative value including zero, and Factor > 0

Cauchy Distribution or Lorentzian Distribution

or

Breit–Wigner Distribution

The Cauchy distribution, also called the Lorentzian distribution or Breit–Wigner distribution, is a continuous distribution describing resonance behavior. It also describes the distribution of horizontal distances at which a line segment tilted at a random angle cuts the x-axis.

The mathematical construct for the Cauchy or Lorentzian distribution is as follows:

$$f(x) = \frac{1}{\pi} \frac{\gamma/2}{(x-m)^2 + \gamma^2/4}$$

The Cauchy distribution is a special case where it does not have any theoretical moments (mean, standard deviation, skewness, and kurtosis) as they are all undefined.

Mode location (m) and scale (γ) are the only two parameters in this distribution. The location parameter specifies the peak or mode of the distribution while the scale parameter specifies the half-width at half-maximum of the distribution. In addition, the mean and variance of a Cauchy or Lorentzian distribution are undefined.

Also, the Cauchy distribution is the Student's t-distribution with only 1 degree of freedom. This distribution is also constructed by taking the ratio of two standard-normal distributions (normal distributions with a mean of zero and a variance of one) that are independent of one another.

Input requirements: Location can be any value and Scale > 0 and can be any positive value

Chi-Square Distribution

The chi-square distribution is a probability distribution used predominantly in hypothesis testing, and it is related to the gamma distribution and the standard-normal distribution. For instance, the sums of independent normal distributions are distributed as a chi-square (χ^2) with k degrees of freedom:

$$Z_1^2 + Z_2^2 + \ldots + Z_k^2 \overset{d}{\sim} \chi_k^2$$

The mathematical constructs for the chi-square distribution are as follows:

$$f(x) = \frac{2^{-k/2}}{\Gamma(k/2)} x^{k/2-1} e^{-x/2} \textit{ for all } x > 0$$

$Mean = k$

$Standard\ Deviation = \sqrt{2k}$

$Skewness = 2\sqrt{\frac{2}{k}}$

$Excess\ Kurtosis = \frac{12}{k}$

Γ is the gamma function. Degrees of freedom k is the only distributional parameter.

The chi-square distribution can also be modeled using a gamma distribution by setting the shape parameter $= \frac{k}{2}$ and scale $= 2S^2$ where S is the scale.

Input requirements: Degrees of freedom > 1 and integer < 1000

Cosine Distribution

The cosine distribution looks like a logistic distribution where the median value between the minimum and maximum has the highest peak or mode, carrying the maximum probability of occurrence, while the extreme tails close to the minimum and maximum values have lower probabilities. Minimum and maximum are the distributional parameters.

The mathematical constructs for the cosine distribution are shown below:

$$f(x) = \begin{cases} \frac{1}{2b} Cos\left[\frac{x-a}{b}\right] & for\ Min \le x \le Max \\ 0 & otherwise \end{cases}$$

$$where\ a = \frac{Min + Max}{2} \quad and\ b = \frac{Max - Min}{\pi}$$

$$F(x) = \begin{cases} \frac{1}{2}\left[1 + Sin\left(\frac{x-a}{b}\right)\right] & for\ Min \le x \le Max \\ 1 & for\ x > Max \end{cases}$$

$$Mean = \frac{Min+Max}{2}$$

$$Standard\ Deviation = \sqrt{\frac{(Max-Min)^2(\pi^2-8)}{4\pi^2}}$$

$$Skewness = 0$$

$$Excess\ Kurtosis = \frac{6(90-\pi^4)}{5(\pi^2-6)^2}$$

Minimum and maximum are the distributional parameters.

Input requirements: *Maximum > minimum* (either input parameter can be positive, negative, or zero)

Double Log Distribution

The double log distribution looks like the Cauchy distribution where the central tendency is peaked and carries the maximum value probability density but declines faster the further away from the center it gets, creating a symmetrical distribution with an extreme peak in between the minimum and maximum values. Minimum and maximum are the distributional parameters.

The mathematical constructs for the double log distribution are shown below:

$$f(x) = \begin{cases} \frac{-1}{2b} \ln\left(\frac{|x-a|}{b}\right) & for\ Min \leq x \leq Max \\ 0 & otherwise \end{cases}$$

$$where\ a = \frac{Min + Max}{2}\ and\ b = \frac{Max - Min}{2}$$

$$F(x) = \begin{cases} \frac{1}{2} - \left(\frac{|x-a|}{2b}\right)\left[1 - \ln\left(\frac{|x-a|}{b}\right)\right] & for\ Min \leq x \leq a \\ \frac{1}{2} + \left(\frac{|x-a|}{2b}\right)\left[1 - \ln\left(\frac{|x-a|}{b}\right)\right] & for\ a \leq x \leq Max \end{cases}$$

$$Mean = \frac{Min+Max}{2}$$

$$Standard\ Deviation = \sqrt{\frac{(Max-Min)^2}{36}}$$

$$Skewness = 0$$

Excess Kurtosis is a complex function

Minimum and maximum are the distributional parameters.

Input requirements: *Maximum > minimum* (either input parameter can be positive, negative, or zero)

Erlang Distribution

The Erlang distribution is the same as the gamma distribution with the requirement that the alpha or shape parameter must be a positive integer. An example application of the Erlang distribution is the calibration of the rate of transition of elements through a system of compartments. Such systems are widely used in biology and ecology (e.g., in epidemiology, an individual may progress at an exponential rate from being healthy to becoming a disease carrier and continue exponentially from being a carrier to being infectious). Alpha (also known as shape) and beta (also known as scale) are the distributional parameters.

The mathematical constructs for the Erlang distribution are shown below:

$$f(x) = \begin{cases} \dfrac{\left(\frac{x}{\beta}\right)^{\alpha-1} e^{-x/\beta}}{\beta(\alpha-1)} & for \ x \geq 0 \\ 0 & otherwise \end{cases}$$

$$F(x) = \begin{cases} 1 - e^{-x/\beta} \sum_{i=0}^{\alpha-1} \dfrac{(x/\beta)^i}{i!} & for \ x \geq 0 \\ 0 & otherwise \end{cases}$$

$Mean = \alpha\beta$

$Standard \ Deviation = \sqrt{\alpha\beta^2}$

$Skewness = \dfrac{2}{\sqrt{\alpha}}$

$Excess \ Kurtosis = \dfrac{6}{\alpha} - 3$

Alpha and beta are the distributional parameters.

Input requirements: *Alpha (shape)* > 0 and is an integer and *Beta (scale)* > 0

Exponential Distribution

The exponential distribution is widely used to describe events recurring at random points in time, such as the time between failures of electronic equipment or the time between arrivals at a service booth. It is related to the Poisson distribution, which describes the number of occurrences of an event in a given interval of time. An important characteristic of the exponential distribution is the *memoryless* property, which means that the future lifetime of a given object has the same distribution, regardless of the time it existed. In other words, time has no effect on future outcomes.

The mathematical constructs for the exponential distribution are as follows:

$f(x) = \lambda e^{-\lambda x}$ for $x \geq 0$; $\lambda > 0$

$Mean = \dfrac{1}{\lambda}$

$Standard \ Deviation = \dfrac{1}{\lambda}$

Skewness = 2 (this value applies to all success rate λ inputs)

Excess Kurtosis = 6 (this value applies to all success rate λ inputs)

Success rate (λ) is the only distributional parameter. The number of successful trials is denoted x. The exponential distribution describes the amount of time between occurrences.

Input requirements: *Rate* > 0 and ≤ 300

Exponential 2 Distribution

The exponential 2 distribution uses the same constructs as the original exponential distribution but adds a location or shift parameter. The exponential distribution starts from a minimum value of 0, whereas this exponential 2, or shifted exponential, distribution shifts the starting location to any other value.

Rate, or lambda, and location, or shift, are the distributional parameters.

Input requirements: *Rate (lambda)* > 0 and Location can be any positive or negative value including zero

Extreme Value or Gumbel Distribution

The extreme value distribution (Type 1) is commonly used to describe the largest value of a response over a period of time, for example, extreme losses in investment portfolios, extreme stock price movements, flood flows, rainfall, and earthquakes. Other applications include the breaking strengths of materials, construction design, and aircraft loads and tolerances. The extreme value distribution is also known as the Gumbel distribution.

The mathematical constructs for the extreme value distribution are as follows:

$$f(x) = \frac{1}{\beta} z e^{-z} \text{ where } z = e^{\frac{x-m}{\beta}} \text{ for } \beta > 0; \text{ and any value of } x \text{ and } m$$

$$Mean = m + 0.577215\beta$$

$$Standard\ Deviation = \sqrt{\frac{1}{6}\pi^2\beta^2}$$

$$Skewness = \frac{12\sqrt{6}(1.2020569)}{\pi^3} = 1.13955$$

$$Excess\ Kurtosis = 5.4$$

Mode (m) and scale (β) are the distributional parameters.

There are two standard parameters for the extreme value distribution: mode and scale. The mode parameter is the most likely value for the variable (the highest point on the probability distribution). The scale parameter is a number greater than 0. The larger the scale parameter, the greater the variance.

Input requirements: *Mode* can be any value and *Scale* > 0

F-Distribution or Fisher–Snedecor Distribution

The F-distribution, also known as the Fisher–Snedecor distribution, is another continuous distribution used most frequently for hypothesis testing. Specifically, it is used to test the statistical difference between two variances in analysis of variance tests and likelihood ratio tests. The F-distribution with the numerator degree of freedom n and denominator degree of freedom m is related to the chi-square distribution in that:

$$\frac{\chi_n^2/n}{\chi_m^2/m} \overset{d}{\sim} F_{n,m} \text{ or } f(x) = \frac{\Gamma\left(\frac{n+m}{2}\right)\left(\frac{n}{m}\right)^{n/2}x^{n/2-1}}{\Gamma\left(\frac{n}{2}\right)\Gamma\left(\frac{m}{2}\right)\left[x\left(\frac{n}{m}\right)+1\right]^{(n+m)/2}}$$

$$Mean = \frac{m}{m-2}$$

$$Standard\ Deviation = \frac{2m^2(m+n-2)}{n(m-2)^2(m-4)} \text{ for all } m > 4$$

$$Skewness = \frac{2(m+2n-2)}{m-6}\sqrt{\frac{2(m-4)}{n(m+n-2)}}$$

$$Excess\ Kurtosis =$$
$$\frac{12(-16+20m-8m^2+m^3+44n-32mn+5m^2n-22n^2+5mn^2}{n(m-6)(m-8)(n+m-2)}$$

The numerator degree of freedom n and denominator degree of freedom m are the only distributional parameters.

Input requirements: Degrees of freedom numerator and degrees of freedom denominator both > 0 integers

Gamma Distribution (Erlang Distribution)

The gamma distribution applies to a wide range of physical quantities and is related to other distributions: lognormal, exponential, Pascal, Erlang, Poisson, and chi-square. It is used in meteorological processes to represent pollutant concentrations and precipitation quantities. The gamma distribution is also used to measure the time between the occurrences of events when the event process is not completely random. Other applications of the gamma distribution include inventory control, economic theory, and insurance risk theory.

The gamma distribution is most often used as the distribution of the amount of time until the rth occurrence of an event in a Poisson process. When used in this fashion, the three conditions underlying the gamma distribution are:

- The number of possible occurrences in any unit of measurement is not limited to a fixed number.

- The occurrences are independent. The number of occurrences in one unit of measurement does not affect the number of occurrences in other units.

- The average number of occurrences must remain the same from unit to unit.

The mathematical constructs for the gamma distribution are as follows:

$$f(x) = \frac{\left(\frac{x}{\beta}\right)^{\alpha-1} e^{-\frac{x}{\beta}}}{\Gamma(\alpha)\beta} \quad \text{with any value of } \alpha > 0 \text{ and } \beta > 0$$

$$Mean = \alpha\beta$$

$$Standard\ Deviation = \sqrt{\alpha\beta^2}$$

$$Skewness = \frac{2}{\sqrt{\alpha}}$$

$$Excess\ Kurtosis = \frac{6}{\alpha}$$

Shape parameter alpha (α) and scale parameter beta (β) are the distributional parameters, and Γ is the gamma function. When the alpha parameter is a positive integer, the gamma distribution is called the Erlang distribution, used to predict waiting times in queuing systems, where the Erlang distribution is the sum of independent and identically distributed random variables each having a memoryless exponential distribution. Setting n as the number of these random variables, the mathematical construct of the Erlang distribution is:

$$f(x) = \frac{x^{n-1}e^{-x}}{(n-1)!} \text{ for all } x > 0 \text{ and all positive integers of } n$$

Input requirements:

Scale beta > 0 and can be any positive value

Shape alpha ≥ 0.05 and any positive value

Location can be any value

Laplace Distribution

The Laplace distribution is sometimes called the double exponential distribution because it can be constructed with two exponential distributions (with an additional location parameter) spliced together back-to-back, creating an unusual peak in the middle. The probability density function of the Laplace distribution is reminiscent of the normal distribution. However, whereas the normal distribution is expressed in terms of the squared difference from the mean, the Laplace density is expressed in terms of the absolute difference from the mean, making the Laplace distribution's tails fatter than those of the normal distribution. When the location parameter is set to zero, the Laplace distribution's random variable is exponentially distributed with an inverse of the scale parameter. Alpha (also known as location) and beta (also known as scale) are the distributional parameters.

The mathematical constructs for the Laplace distribution are shown below:

$$f(x) = \frac{1}{2\beta} exp\left(-\frac{|x-\alpha|}{\beta}\right)$$

$$F(x) = \begin{cases} \frac{1}{2} exp\left[\frac{x-\alpha}{\beta}\right] & when \; x < \alpha \\ 1 - \frac{1}{2} exp\left[-\frac{x-\alpha}{\beta}\right] & when \; x \geq \alpha \end{cases}$$

Mean = α

Standard Deviation = 1.4142β

Skewness is always equal to 0 as it is a symmetrical distribution

Excess Kurtosis is always equal to 3

Input requirements: *Alpha (location)* can take on any positive or negative value including zero and *Beta (scale)* > 0

Logistic Distribution

The logistic distribution is commonly used to describe growth, that is, the size of a population expressed as a function of a time variable. It also can be used to describe chemical reactions and the course of growth for a population or individual.

The mathematical constructs for the logistic distribution are as follows:

$$f(x) = \frac{e^{\frac{\mu - x}{\alpha}}}{\alpha \left[1 + e^{\frac{\mu - x}{\alpha}}\right]^2} \quad \text{for any value of } \alpha \text{ and } \mu$$

Mean $= \mu$

Standard Deviation $= \sqrt{\frac{1}{3} \pi^2 \alpha^2}$

Skewness = 0 (this applies to all mean and scale inputs)

Excess Kurtosis = 1.2 (this applies to all mean and scale inputs)

Mean (μ) and *scale* (α) are the distributional parameters.

There are two standard parameters for the logistic distribution: mean and scale. The mean parameter is the average value, which for this distribution is the same as the mode, because this distribution is symmetrical. The scale parameter is a number greater than 0. The larger the scale parameter, the greater the variance.

Input requirements:

Scale > 0 and can be any positive value

Mean can be any value

Lognormal Distribution

The lognormal distribution is widely used in situations where values are positively skewed, for example, in financial analysis for security valuation or in real estate for property valuation, and where values cannot fall below zero.

Stock prices are usually positively skewed rather than normally (symmetrically) distributed. Stock prices exhibit this trend because they cannot fall below the lower limit of zero but might increase to any price without limit. Similarly, real estate prices illustrate positive skewness and are lognormally distributed as property values cannot become negative.

The three conditions underlying the lognormal distribution are:

- The uncertain variable can increase without limits but cannot fall below zero.

- The uncertain variable is positively skewed, with most of the values near the lower limit.

- The natural logarithm of the uncertain variable yields a normal distribution.

Generally, if the coefficient of variability is greater than 30%, use a lognormal distribution. Otherwise, use the normal distribution.

The mathematical constructs for the lognormal distribution are as follows:

$$f(x) = \frac{1}{x\sqrt{2\pi}\ln(\sigma)} e^{\frac{-[\ln(x)-\ln(\mu)]^2}{2[\ln(\sigma)]^2}} \quad for\ x > 0;\ \mu > 0\ and\ \sigma > 0$$

$$Mean = exp\left(\mu + \frac{\sigma^2}{2}\right)$$

$$Standard\ Deviation = \sqrt{exp(\sigma^2 + 2\mu)\,[exp(\sigma^2) - 1]}$$

$$Skewness = \left[\sqrt{exp(\sigma^2) - 1}\right](2 + exp(\sigma^2))$$

$$Excess\ Kurtosis = exp\ (4\sigma^2) + 2\,exp\ (3\sigma^2) + 3\,exp\ (2\sigma^2) - 6$$

Mean (μ) and standard deviation (σ) are the distributional parameters.

Input requirements: Mean and standard deviation both > 0 and can be any positive value

Lognormal Parameter Sets: By default, the lognormal distribution uses the arithmetic mean and standard deviation. For applications for which historical data are available, it is more appropriate to use either the logarithmic mean and standard deviation, or the geometric mean and standard deviation.

Lognormal 3 Distribution

The lognormal 3 distribution uses the same constructs as the original lognormal distribution but adds a location, or shift, parameter. The lognormal distribution starts from a minimum value of 0, whereas this lognormal 3, or shifted lognormal, distribution shifts the starting location to any other value.

Mean, standard deviation, and location (shift) are the distributional parameters.

Input requirements:

Mean > 0 and *Standard Deviation* > 0

Location can be any positive or negative value including zero

Normal Distribution

The normal distribution is the most important distribution in probability theory because it describes many natural phenomena, such as people's IQs or heights. Decision makers can use the normal distribution to describe uncertain variables such as the inflation rate or the future price of gasoline.

The three conditions underlying the normal distribution are:

- Some value of the uncertain variable is the most likely (the mean of the distribution).

- The uncertain variable could as likely be above the mean as it could be below the mean (symmetrical about the mean).

- The uncertain variable is more likely in the vicinity of the mean than further away.

The mathematical constructs for the normal distribution are:

$$f(x) = \frac{1}{\sqrt{2\pi}\sigma} e^{\frac{-(x-\mu)^2}{2\sigma^2}} \text{ for all values of } x \text{ and } \mu; \text{ while } \sigma > 0$$

$Mean = \mu$

$Standard\ Deviation = \sigma$

Skewness = 0

Excess Kurtosis = 0

Mean (μ) and *standard deviation* (σ) are the distributional parameters.

Input requirements: *Standard deviation* > 0 and can be any positive value whereas mean can be any value

Parabolic Distribution

The parabolic distribution is a special case of the beta distribution when *Shape* = *Scale* = 2. Values close to the minimum and maximum have low probabilities of occurrence, whereas values between these two extremes have higher probabilities of occurrence. Minimum and maximum are the distributional parameters.

The mathematical constructs for the parabolic distribution are shown below:

$$f(x) = \frac{(x)^{(\alpha-1)}(1-x)^{(\beta-1)}}{\left[\frac{\Gamma(\alpha)\Gamma(\beta)}{\Gamma(\alpha+\beta)}\right]} \quad \text{for } \alpha > 0; \beta > 0; x > 0$$

Whereas the functional form above is for a beta distribution, for a parabolic function, we set *alpha* = *beta* = 2 and a shift of location in minimum, with a multiplicative factor of (*Max* - *Min*).

$$Mean = \frac{Min+Max}{2}$$

$$Standard\ Deviation = \sqrt{\frac{(Max-Min)^2}{20}}$$

Skewness = 0

Excess Kurtosis = −0.8571

Minimum and maximum are the distributional parameters.

Input requirements: *Maximum* > *minimum* (either can be positive, negative, or zero)

Pareto Distribution

The Pareto distribution is widely used for the investigation of distributions associated with such empirical phenomena as city population sizes, the occurrence of natural resources, the size of companies, personal incomes, stock price fluctuations, and error clustering in communication circuits.

The mathematical constructs for the Pareto are as follows:

$$f(x) = \frac{\beta L^\beta}{x^{(1+\beta)}} \quad \text{for } x > L$$

$$Mean = \frac{\beta L}{\beta - 1}$$

$$Standard\ Deviation = \sqrt{\frac{\beta L^2}{(\beta-1)^2 (\beta-2)}}$$

$$Skewness = \sqrt{\frac{\beta-2}{\beta}} \left[\frac{2(\beta+1)}{\beta-3} \right]$$

$$Excess\ Kurtosis = \frac{6(\beta^3 + \beta^2 - 6\beta - 2)}{\beta(\beta-3)(\beta-4)}$$

Location (L) and *shape (β)* are the distributional parameters.

There are two standard parameters for the Pareto distribution: location and shape. The location parameter is the lower bound for the variable. After you select the location parameter, you can estimate the shape parameter. The shape parameter is a number greater than 0, usually greater than 1. The larger the shape parameter, the smaller the variance and the thicker the right tail of the distribution.

Input requirements:

Location > 0 and can be any positive value

Shape ≥ 0.05

Pearson V Distribution

The Pearson V distribution is related to the inverse gamma distribution, where it is the reciprocal of the variable distributed according to the gamma distribution. Pearson V distribution is also used to model time delays where there is almost certainty of some minimum delay and the maximum delay is unbounded; for example, delay in arrival of emergency services and time to repair a machine. Alpha (also known as shape) and beta (also known as scale) are the distributional parameters.

The mathematical constructs for the Pearson V distribution are shown below:

$$f(x) = \frac{x^{-(\alpha+1)}e^{-\beta/x}}{\beta^{-\alpha}\Gamma(\alpha)}$$

$$F(x) = \frac{\Gamma(\alpha,\beta/x)}{\Gamma(\alpha)}$$

$$Mean = \frac{\beta}{\alpha-1}$$

$$Standard\ Deviation = \sqrt{\frac{\beta^2}{(\alpha-1)^2(\alpha-2)}}$$

$$Skewness = \frac{4\sqrt{\alpha-2}}{\alpha-3}$$

$$Excess\ Kurtosis = \frac{30\alpha-66}{(\alpha-3)(\alpha-4)} - 3$$

Input requirements: *Alpha (shape)* > 0 and *Beta (scale)* > 0

Pearson VI Distribution

The Pearson VI distribution is related to the gamma distribution where it is the rational function of two variables distributed according to two gamma distributions. Alpha 1 (also known as shape 1), alpha 2 (also known as shape 2), and beta (also known as scale) are the distributional parameters. The mathematical constructs for the Pearson VI distribution are shown below:

$$f(x) = \frac{(x/\beta)^{\alpha_1-1}}{\beta\ B(\alpha_1,\alpha_2)[1+(x/\beta)]^{\alpha_1+\alpha_2}}$$

$$F(x) = F_B\left(\frac{x}{x+\beta}\right)$$

$$Mean = \frac{\beta\alpha_1}{\alpha_2-1}$$

$$Standard\ Deviation = \sqrt{\frac{\beta^2\alpha_1(\alpha_1+\alpha_2-1)}{(\alpha_2-1)^2(\alpha_2-2)}}$$

$$Skewness = 2\sqrt{\frac{\alpha_2-2}{\alpha_1(\alpha_1+\alpha_2-1)}}\left[\frac{2\alpha_1+\alpha_2-1}{\alpha_2-3}\right]$$

$$Excess\ Kurtosis = \frac{3(\alpha_2-2)}{(\alpha_2-3)(\alpha_2-4)}\left[\frac{2(\alpha_2-1)^2}{\alpha_1(\alpha_1+\alpha_2-1)} + (\alpha_2 + 5)\right] - 3$$

Input requirements: *Alpha 1 (shape 1)* > 0; *Alpha 2 (shape 2)* > 0; and *Beta (scale)* > 0

PERT Distribution

The PERT distribution is widely used in project and program management to define the worst-case, nominal-case, and best-case scenarios of project completion time. It is related to the beta and triangular distributions. PERT distribution can be used to identify risks in project and cost models based on the likelihood of meeting targets and goals across any number of project components using minimum, most likely, and maximum values, but it is designed to generate a distribution that more closely resembles realistic probability distributions. The PERT distribution can provide a close fit to the normal or lognormal distributions. Like the triangular distribution, the PERT distribution emphasizes the *most likely* value over the minimum and maximum estimates. However, unlike the triangular distribution, the PERT distribution constructs a smooth curve that places progressively more emphasis on values around (near) the most likely value in favor of values around the edges. In practice, this means that we *trust* the estimate for the most likely value, and we believe that even if it is not exactly accurate (as estimates seldom are), we have an expectation that the resulting value will be close to that estimate. Assuming that many real-world phenomena are normally distributed, the appeal of the PERT distribution is that it produces a curve similar to the normal curve in shape, without knowing the precise parameters of the related normal curve. Minimum, most likely, and maximum are the distributional parameters.

The mathematical constructs for the PERT distribution are shown below:

$$f(x) = \frac{(x-Min)^{A1-1}(Max-x)^{A2-1}}{B(A1,A2)(Max-Min)^{A1+A2-1}}$$

$$where\ A1 = 6\left[\frac{\frac{Min+4(Likely)+Max}{6}-Min}{Max-Min}\right]$$

$$and\ A2 = 6\left[\frac{Max-\frac{Min+4(Likely)+Max}{6}}{Max-Min}\right]$$

$$and\ B\ is\ the\ Beta\ function$$

$$Mean = \frac{Min+4Mode+Max}{6}$$

$$Standard\ Deviation = \sqrt{\frac{(\mu-Min)(Max-\mu)}{7}}$$

$$Skewness = \sqrt{\frac{7}{(\mu-Min)(Max-\mu)}}\left(\frac{Min+Max-2\mu}{4}\right)$$

Excess Kurtosis is a complex function

Input requirements: *Min* $\leq$ *Most Likely* $\leq$ *Max* and can be positive, negative, or zero

Power Distribution

The power distribution is related to the exponential distribution in that the probability of small outcomes is large but exponentially decreases as the outcome value increases. Alpha (also known as shape) is the only distributional parameter. The mathematical constructs for the power distribution are shown below:

$$f(x) = \alpha x^{\alpha-1}$$

$$F(x) = x^{\alpha}$$

$$Mean = \frac{\alpha}{1+\alpha}$$

$$Standard\ Deviation = \sqrt{\frac{\alpha}{(1+\alpha)^2(2+\alpha)}}$$

$$Skewness = \sqrt{\frac{\alpha+2}{\alpha}}\left(\frac{2(\alpha-1)}{\alpha+3}\right)$$

Excess Kurtosis is complex and cannot be easily computed

Input requirements: *Alpha* > 0

Power 3 Distribution

The power 3 distribution uses the same constructs as the original power distribution but adds a location, or shift, parameter and a multiplicative factor parameter. The power distribution starts from a minimum value of 0, whereas this power 3, or shifted multiplicative power, distribution shifts the starting location to any other value.

Alpha, location or shift, and factor are the distributional parameters.

Input requirements:

Alpha > 0.05

Location, or shift, can be any value including zero

Factor > 0

Student's t-Distribution

The Student's t-distribution is the most widely used distribution in hypothesis testing. This distribution is used to estimate the mean of a normally distributed population when the sample size is small, and is used to test the statistical significance of the difference between two sample means or confidence intervals for small sample sizes.

The mathematical constructs for the t-distribution are as follows:

$$f(t) = \frac{\Gamma\left[(r+1)/2\right]}{\sqrt{r\pi}\,\Gamma[r/2]} \left(1 + t^2/r\right)^{-(r+1)/2}$$

where $t = \frac{x-\bar{x}}{s}$ and Γ is the gamma function

Mean $= 0$ (all degrees of freedom r except if the distribution is shifted to another nonzero central location)

Standard Deviation $= \sqrt{\dfrac{r}{r-2}}$

Skewness $= 0$ (this applies to all degrees of freedom r)

Excess Kurtosis $= \dfrac{6}{r-4}$ for all $r > 4$

Degree of freedom r is the only distributional parameter.

The t-distribution is related to the F-distribution as follows: the square of a value of t with r degrees of freedom is distributed as F with 1 and r degrees of freedom. The overall shape of the probability density function of the t-distribution also resembles the bell shape of a normally distributed variable with mean 0 and variance 1, except that it is a bit lower and wider or is leptokurtic (fat tails at the ends and peaked center). As the number of degrees of freedom grows (say, above 30), the t-distribution approaches the normal distribution with mean 0 and variance 1.

Input requirements: *Degrees of freedom* ≥ 1 and must be an integer

Triangular Distribution

The triangular distribution describes a situation where you know the minimum, maximum, and most likely values to occur. For example, you could describe the number of cars sold per week when past sales show the minimum, maximum, and usual number of cars sold.

The three conditions underlying the triangular distribution are:

- The minimum number of items is fixed.

- The maximum number of items is fixed.

- The most likely number of items falls between the minimum and maximum values, forming a triangular-shaped distribution, which shows that values near the minimum and maximum are less likely to occur than those near the most-likely value.

The mathematical constructs for the triangular distribution are as follows:

$$f(x) = \begin{cases} \dfrac{2(x - Min)}{(Max - Min)(Likely - min)} & \text{for } Min < x < Likely \\ \dfrac{2(Max - x)}{(Max - Min)(Max - Likely)} & \text{for } Likely < x < Max \end{cases}$$

$$Mean = \frac{1}{3}(Min + Likely + Max)$$

$$Standard\ Deviation =$$
$$\sqrt{\frac{1}{18}(Min^2 + Likely^2 + Max^2 - MinMax - MinLikely - MaxLikely)}$$

$$Skewness = \frac{\sqrt{2}(Min+Max-2Likely)(2Min-Max-Likely)(Min-2Max+Likely)}{5(Min^2+Max^2+Likely^2-MinMax-MinLikely-MaxLikely)^{3/2}}$$

$$Excess\ Kurtosis = -0.6$$

Minimum (Min), *most likely (Likely)*, and *maximum (Max)* are the parameters.

Input requirements:

Min ≤ *Most Likely* ≤ *Max* and can take any value

However, *Min* < *Max* and can take any value

Uniform Distribution

With the uniform distribution, all values fall between the minimum and maximum and occur with equal likelihood.

The three conditions underlying the uniform distribution are:

- The minimum value is fixed.

- The maximum value is fixed.

- All values between the minimum and maximum occur with equal likelihood.

The mathematical constructs for the uniform distribution are as follows:

$$f(x) = \frac{1}{Max-Min} \text{ for all values such that } Min < Max$$

$$Mean = \frac{Min+Max}{2}$$

$$Standard\ Deviation = \sqrt{\frac{(Max-Min)^2}{12}}$$

$$Skewness = 0$$

$$Excess\ Kurtosis = -1.2 \text{ (applies to all inputs of } Min \text{ and } Max)$$

The distributional parameters are Maximum and Minimum.

Input requirements: $Min < Max$ and can take any value

Weibull Distribution (Rayleigh Distribution)

The Weibull distribution describes data resulting from life and fatigue tests. It is commonly used to describe failure time in reliability studies as well as the breaking strengths of materials in reliability and quality control tests. Weibull distributions are also used to represent various physical quantities, such as wind speed. The Weibull distribution is a family of distributions that can assume the properties of several other distributions. For example, depending on the shape parameter you define, the Weibull distribution can be used to model the exponential and Rayleigh distributions, among others. The Weibull distribution is very flexible. When the Weibull shape parameter is equal to 1.0, the Weibull distribution is identical to the exponential distribution. The Weibull location parameter lets you set up an exponential distribution to start at a location other than 0.0. When the shape parameter is less than 1.0, the Weibull distribution becomes a steeply declining curve. A manufacturer might find this effect useful in describing part failures during a burn-in period.

The mathematical constructs for the Weibull distribution are as follows:

$$f(x) = \frac{\alpha}{\beta}\left[\frac{x}{\beta}\right]^{\alpha-1} e^{-\left(\frac{x}{\beta}\right)^{\alpha}}$$

$Mean = \beta\Gamma(1 + \alpha^{-1})$

$Standard\ Deviation = \beta^2[\Gamma(1 + 2\alpha^{-1}) - \Gamma^2(1 + \alpha^{-1})]$

$Skewness = \dfrac{2\Gamma^3(1+\beta^{-1})-3\Gamma(1+\beta^{-1})\Gamma(1+2\beta^{-1})+\Gamma(1+3\beta^{-1})}{[\Gamma(1+2\beta^{-1})-\Gamma^2(1+\beta^{-1})]^{3/2}}$

$Excess\ Kurtosis =$
$\dfrac{-6\Gamma^4(1+\beta^{-1})+12\Gamma^2(1+\beta^{-1})\Gamma(1+2\beta^{-1})-3\Gamma^2(1+2\beta^{-1})-4\Gamma(1+\beta^{-1})\Gamma(1+3\beta^{-1})+\Gamma(1+4\beta^{-1})}{[\Gamma(1+2\beta^{-1})-\Gamma^2(1+\beta^{-1})]^2}$

Location (L), *shape* (α), and *scale* (β) are the distributional parameters, and Γ is the *Gamma* function.

Input requirements:

Scale > 0 and can be any positive value

Shape ≥ 0.05

Location can take on any value

Weibull 3 Distribution

The Weibull 3 distribution uses the same constructs as the original Weibull distribution but adds a location, or shift, parameter. The Weibull distribution starts from a minimum value of 0, whereas this Weibull 3, or shifted Weibull, distribution shifts the starting location to any other value.

Alpha, beta, and location or shift are the distributional parameters.

Input requirements:

Alpha (shape) ≥ 0.05

Beta (central location scale) > 0 and can be any positive value

Location can be any positive or negative value including zero

6

FITTING PROBABILITY DISTRIBUTIONS

DISTRIBUTIONAL FITTING: SINGLE VARIABLE AND MULTIPLE VARIABLES

Another powerful simulation tool is distributional fitting; that is, how does an analyst or engineer determine which distribution to use for a particular input variable? What are the relevant distributional parameters? If no historical data exist, then the analyst must make assumptions about the variables in question. One approach is to use the Delphi method, where a group of experts are tasked with estimating the behavior of each variable. For instance, a group of mechanical engineers can be tasked with evaluating the extreme possibilities of a spring coil's diameter through rigorous experimentation or guesstimates. These values can be used as the variable's input parameters (e.g., uniform distribution with extreme values between 0.5 and 1.2). When testing is not possible (e.g., market share and revenue growth rate), management can still make estimates of potential outcomes and provide the best-case, most-likely case, and worst-case scenarios, whereupon a triangular or custom distribution can be created.

However, if reliable historical data are available, distributional fitting can be accomplished. Assuming that historical patterns hold and that history tends to repeat itself, then historical data can be used to find the best-fitting distribution with their relevant parameters to better define the variables to be simulated. Figures 6.1, 6.2, and 6.3

illustrate a distributional-fitting example. The demonstration that follows uses the *Data Fitting* file in the examples folder.

Use the following steps to perform a distributional fitting model:

- Open a spreadsheet with existing data for fitting (e.g., use the *Risk Simulator | Example Models | 06 Data Fitting*).

- Select the data you wish to fit not including the variable name (data should be in a single column with multiple rows).

- Select *Risk Simulator | Analytical Tools | 11 Distributional Fitting (Single-Variable)*.

- Select the specific distributions you wish to fit to or keep the default where all distributions are selected and click *OK* (Figure 6.1).

- Review the results of the fit, choose the relevant distribution you want, and click *OK* (Figure 6.2).

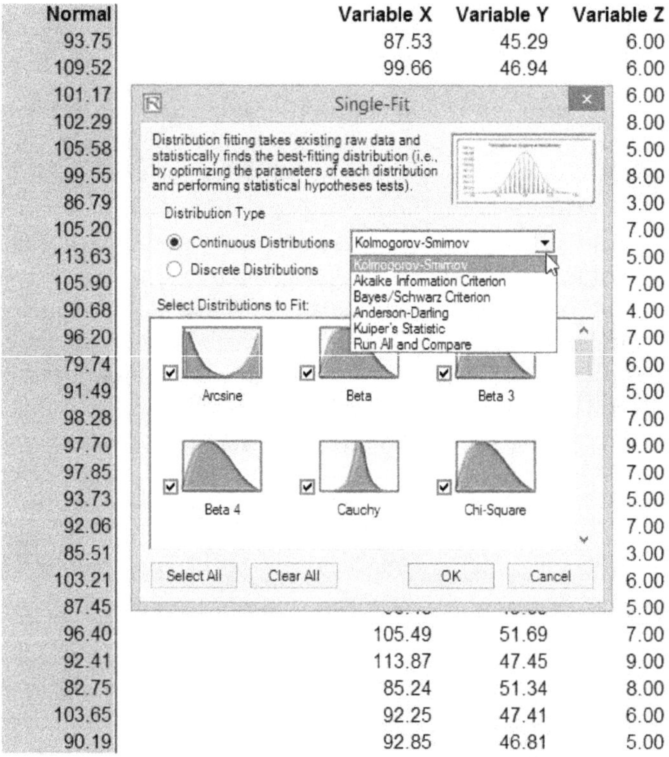

Figure 6.1: Single Variable Distributional Fitting

The null hypothesis (H_o) being tested is such that the fitted distribution is the same distribution as the population from which the sample data to be fitted come. Thus, if the computed p-value is lower than a critical alpha level (typically 0.10 or 0.05), then the distribution is the wrong distribution. Conversely, the *higher the p-value, the better the distribution fits the data*. Roughly, you can think of p-value as a *percentage explained*, that is, if the p-value is 0.9996 (Figure 6.2), then setting a normal distribution with a mean of 100.67 and a standard deviation of 10.40 explains about 99.96% of the variation in the data, indicating an especially good fit. The data was from a 1,000-trial simulation in Risk Simulator based on a normal distribution with a mean of 100 and a standard deviation of 10. Because only 1,000 trials were simulated, the resulting distribution is fairly close to the specified distributional parameters, and in this case, about a 99.96% precision.

Both the results (Figure 6.2) and the report (Figure 6.3) show the test statistic, p-value, theoretical statistics (based on the selected distribution), empirical statistics (based on the raw data), the original data (to maintain a record of the data used), and the assumption complete with the relevant distributional parameters (i.e., if you selected the option to automatically generate assumption and if a simulation profile already exists). The results also rank all the selected distributions and how well they fit the data.

Distribution Fitting Result – □ ✕

Distribution	Test Statistics	P-Value	Rank
Normal	0.02	99.96 %	1
Gamma	0.03	98.83 %	2
Lognormal	0.03	98.37 %	3
Lognormal 3	0.03	98.33 %	4
Logistic	0.03	97.19 %	5
Parabolic	0.04	88.55 %	6
Laplace	0.05	76.07 %	7
Gumbel Minimum	0.05	73.91 %	8
Gumbel Maximum	0.05	57.47 %	9
Double Log	0.06	44.25 %	10
Cauchy	0.07	26.58 %	11
Triangular	0.08	15.90 %	12
Chi-Square	0.10	3.11 %	13
Cosine	0.11	1.30 %	14
Exponential 2	0.12	0.67 %	15
Pareto	0.15	0.04 %	16

Statistical Summary

Theoretical vs. Empirical Distribution

Normal
Mean = 100.67
Standard Deviation = 10.40

Kolmogorov-Smirnov Test Statistic
Test Statistic: 0.02
P-Value: 99.96 %

	Actual	Theoretical
Mean	100.61	100.67
Stdev	10.31	10.40
Skewness	0.01	0.00
Kurtosis	-0.13	0.00

☑ Automatically Generate Assumption   OK   Cancel

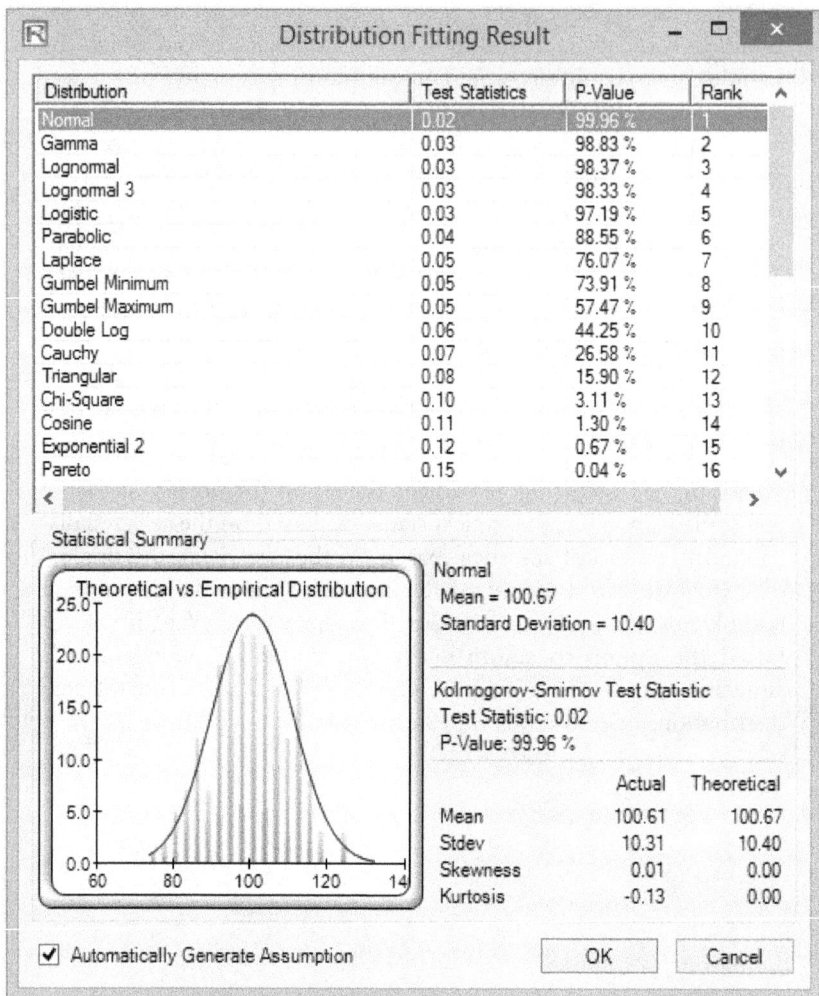

Figure 6.2: Distributional Fitting Result

Statistical Summary

		Actual	Theoretical
Fitted Assumption	100.61		
Fitted Distribution **Normal**			
Mean	100.67		
Standard Deviation	10.40		
Kolmogorov-Smirnov Statistic	0.02		
P-Value for Test Statistic	0.9996		
Mean		100.61	100.67
Standard Deviation		10.31	10.40
Skewness		0.01	0.00
Excess Kurtosis		-0.13	0.00

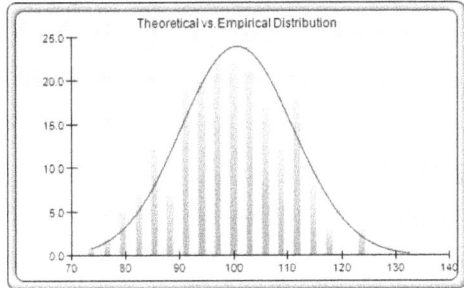

Theoretical vs. Empirical Distribution

Original Fitted Data

73.53	78.21	78.52	79.50	79.72	79.74	81.56	82.08	82.68	82.75	83.34	83.64	84.09
84.66	85.00	85.35	85.51	86.04	86.79	86.82	86.91	87.02	87.03	87.45	87.53	87.66
88.05	88.45	88.51	89.95	90.19	90.54	90.68	90.96	91.25	91.49	91.56	91.94	92.06
92.36	92.41	92.45	92.70	92.80	92.84	93.21	93.26	93.48	93.73	93.75	93.77	93.82
94.00	94.15	94.51	94.57	94.64	94.69	94.95	95.57	95.62	95.71	95.78	95.83	95.97
96.20	96.24	96.40	96.43	96.47	96.81	96.88	97.00	97.07	97.21	97.23	97.48	97.70
97.77	97.85	98.15	98.17	98.24	98.28	98.32	98.33	98.35	98.65	99.03	99.27	99.46
99.47	99.55	99.73	99.96	100.08	100.24	100.36	100.42	100.44	100.48	100.49	100.83	101.17
101.28	101.34	101.45	101.46	101.55	101.73	101.74	101.81	102.29	102.55	102.58	102.60	102.70
103.17	103.21	103.22	103.32	103.34	103.45	103.65	103.66	103.72	103.81	103.90	103.99	104.46
104.57	104.76	105.20	105.44	105.50	105.52	105.58	105.66	105.87	105.90	105.90	106.29	106.35
106.59	107.01	107.68	107.70	107.93	108.17	108.20	108.34	108.42	108.43	108.49	108.70	109.15
109.22	109.35	109.52	109.75	110.04	110.16	110.25	110.54	111.05	111.06	111.44	111.76	111.90
111.95	112.07	112.19	112.29	112.32	112.42	112.48	112.85	112.92	113.50	113.59	113.63	113.70
114.13	114.14	114.21	114.91	114.95	115.40	115.58	115.66	116.58	116.98	117.60	118.67	119.24
119.52	124.14	124.16	124.39	132.30								

Figure 6.3: Distributional Fitting Report

FITTING MULTIPLE VARIABLES

For fitting multiple variables, the process is fairly similar to fitting individual variables. However, the data should be arranged in columns (i.e., each variable is arranged as a column) and all the variables are fitted. The same analysis is performed when fitting multiple variables as when single variables are fitted. The difference here is that only the final report will be generated and you do not get to review each variable's distributional rankings. If the rankings are important, run the single variable fitting procedure instead, on one variable at a time.

- Open a spreadsheet with existing data for fitting (e.g., use the *Risk Simulator | Example Models | 06 Data Fitting*).

- Select the data you wish to fit (data should be in multiple columns with multiple rows).

- Select *Risk Simulator* | *Analytical Tools* | *12 Distributional Fitting (Multi-Variable)*. Review the data, choose the types of distributions you want to fit to, and click *OK*.

Notice that the statistical ranking methods used in the distributional fitting routines in the examples above are the Chi-Square test and Kolmogorov–Smirnov test (other distributional fitting methods are discussed in the next section). The former is used to test discrete distributions and the latter, continuous distributions. Briefly, a hypothesis test coupled with the maximum likelihood procedure with an internal optimization routine is used to find the best-fitting parameters on each distribution tested and the results are ranked from the best fit to the worst fit. There are other distributional fitting tests such as the Shapiro-Wilks, and so on. However, these tests are very sensitive parametric tests and are highly inappropriate in Monte Carlo risk simulation distribution-fitting routines when different distributions are being tested. Due to their parametric requirements, these tests are most suited for testing normal distributions and distributions with normal-like behaviors (e.g., binomial distribution with a high number of trials and symmetrical probabilities) and will provide less accurate results when performed on non-normal distributions. Take great care when using such parametric tests. The Kolmogorov–Smirnov and Chi-Square tests employed in Risk Simulator are nonparametric and semiparametric in nature and are better suited for fitting normal and non-normal distributions. Additional distributional fitting methods are discussed next.

DISTRIBUTIONAL FITTING ALGORITHMS

Generally speaking, distributional fitting answers the questions: Which distribution does an analyst or engineer use for a particular input variable in a model? What are the relevant distributional parameters? Following are additional methods of distributional fitting available in Risk Simulator:

- Akaike Information Criterion (AIC). Rewards goodness-of-fit but also includes a penalty that is an increasing function of the number of estimated parameters (although AIC penalizes the number of parameters less strongly than other methods).

- Anderson–Darling (AD). When applied to testing if a normal distribution adequately describes a set of data, it is one of the most powerful statistical tools for detecting departures from normality and is powerful for testing normal tails. However, in non-normal distributions, this test lacks power compared to others.

- Kolmogorov–Smirnov (KS). A nonparametric test for the equality of continuous probability distributions that can be used to compare a sample with a reference probability distribution, making it useful for testing abnormally shaped distributions and non-normal distributions.

- Kuiper's Statistic (K). Related to the KS test making it as sensitive in the tails as at the median and also making it invariant under cyclic transformations of the independent variable, rendering it invaluable when testing for cyclic variations over time. In comparison, the AD test provides equal sensitivity at the tails as the median, but it does not provide the cyclic invariance.

- Schwarz/Bayes Information Criterion (SC/BIC). The SC/BIC test introduces a penalty term for the number of parameters in the model with a larger penalty than AIC.

The null hypothesis being tested is such that the fitted distribution is the same distribution as the population from which the sample data to be fitted comes. Thus, if the computed p-value is lower than a critical alpha level (typically 0.10 or 0.05), then the distribution is the wrong distribution (reject the null hypothesis). Conversely, the higher the p-value, the better the distribution fits the data (do not reject the null hypothesis, which means the fitted distribution is the correct distribution, or null hypothesis of H_0: *Error = 0*, where error is defined as the difference between the empirical data and the theoretical distribution). Roughly, you can think of p-value as a percentage explained; that is, for example, if the computed p-value of a fitted normal distribution is 0.9996, then setting a normal distribution with the fitted mean and standard deviation explains about 99.96% of the variation in the data, indicating an especially good fit. Both the results and the report show the test statistic, p-value, theoretical statistics (based on the selected distribution), empirical statistics (based on the raw data), the original data (to maintain a record of the data used), and the assumptions complete with the relevant distributional parameters (i.e., if you selected the option to automatically generate assumptions and if a simulation profile already exists). The results also rank all the selected distributions and how well they fit the data.

PERCENTILE DISTRIBUTIONAL FITTING TOOL

The Percentile Distributional Fitting tool in Risk Simulator is an alternate way of fitting probability distributions. There are several related tools and each has its own uses and advantages:

- Distributional Fitting (Percentiles). Uses an alternate method of entry (percentiles and first/second moment combinations) to find the best-fitting parameters of a specified distribution without the need for having raw data. This method is suitable for use when there are insufficient data or only when percentiles and moments are available, or as a means to recover the entire distribution with only two or three data points but the distribution type needs to be assumed or known.

- Distributional Fitting (Single Variable). Uses statistical methods to fit your raw data to all 50 distributions to find the best-fitting distribution and its input parameters. Multiple data points are required for a good fit, and the distribution type may or may not be known ahead of time.

- Distributional Fitting (Multiple Variables). Uses statistical methods to fit your raw data on multiple variables at the same time. This method uses the same algorithms as the single-variable fitting, but incorporates a pairwise correlation matrix between the variables. Multiple data points are required for a good fit, and the distribution type may or may not be known ahead of time.

- Custom Distribution (Set Assumption). Uses nonparametric resampling techniques to generate a custom distribution with the existing raw data and to simulate the distribution based on this empirical distribution. Fewer data points are required, and the distribution type is not known ahead of time. This tool is also suitable for subject matter expert (SME) estimates, the Delphi method, and management assumptions.

Click on *Risk Simulator* | *Analytical Tools* | *Distributional Fitting (Percentiles)*, choose the probability distribution and types of inputs you wish to use, enter the parameters, and click *Run* to obtain the results. Review the fitted R-square results and compare the empirical versus theoretical fitting results to determine if your distribution is a good fit. For instance, Figure 6.4 shows how a normal distribution can be fitted by simply using its percentiles. In this example, the 15th percentile has a value of 25.4 and the 85th percentile has a value of 49.5, yielding a 100% fit on a normal distribution with a mean of 37.4 and standard deviation of 11.6.

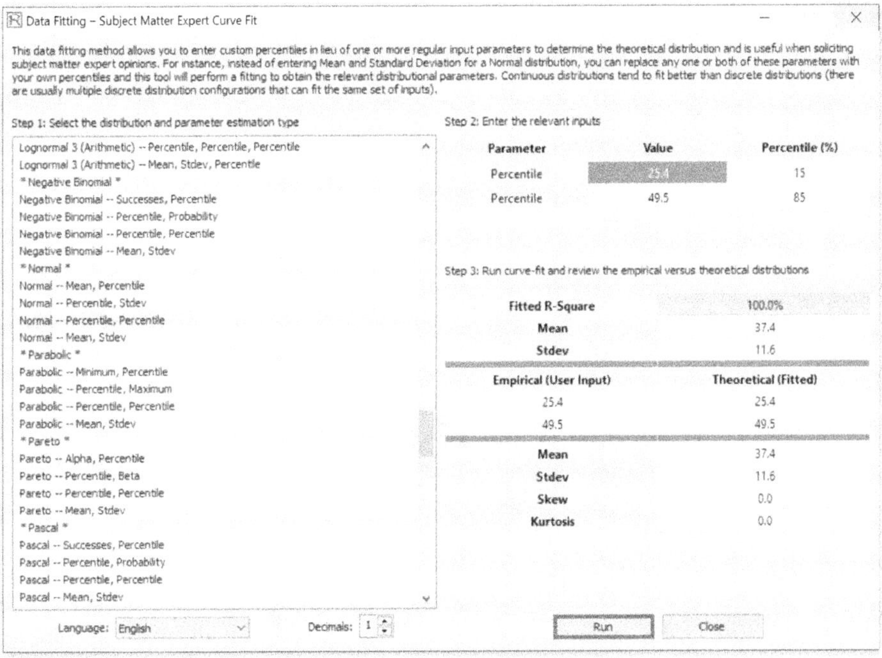

Figure 6.4: Percentile Fitting Technique

7

COPULAS AND CORRELATING DISTRIBUTIONS

This chapter explains the basics of Convolution Theory and Copula Theory as they apply to probability distributions and stochastic modeling, both in theory and practice. It attempts to show that, in theory, convolution and copulas are elegant and critical in solving basic distributional moments but when it comes to practical applications, these theories are unwieldy and mathematically intractable. Consequently, it is necessary to run empirical Monte Carlo simulations, where the results of said empirical simulations approach the theoretically predicted results at the limit, allowing practitioners a powerful practical toolkit for modeling.

Many probability distributions are both flexible and interchangeable. For example:

- Arcsine and parabolic distributions are special cases of the beta distribution.

- Binomial and Poisson distributions approach the normal distribution at the limit.

- Binomial distribution is a Bernoulli distribution with multiple trials.

- Chi-square distribution is the squared sum of multiple normal distributions.

- Discrete uniform distributions' sum (12 or more) approaches the normal distribution.

- Erlang distribution is a special case of the gamma distribution when the alpha shape parameter is positive.

- Exponential distribution is the inverse of the Poisson distribution on a continuous basis.

- F-distribution is the ratio of two chi-square distributions.

- Gamma distribution is related to the lognormal, exponential, Pascal, Erlang, Poisson, and chi-square distributions.

- Laplace distribution comprises two exponential distributions in one.

- Lognormal distribution's logarithmic values approach the normal distribution.

- Pascal distribution is a shifted negative binomial distribution.

- Pearson V distribution is the inverse of the gamma distribution.

- Pearson VI distribution is the ratio of two gamma distributions.

- PERT distribution is a modified beta distribution.

- Rayleigh distribution is a modified Weibull distribution.

- T-distribution with high degrees of freedom (>30) approaches the normal distribution.

CONVOLUTION

Mathematicians came up with the distributions listed above through the use of convolution, among other methods. As a quick introduction, if there are two independent and identically distributed (*i.i.d.*) random variables, X and Y, and where their respectively known probability density functions (PDF) are $f_X(x)$ and $f_Y(y)$, we can then generate a new probability distribution by combining X and Y using basic summation, multiplication, and division. Some examples are listed above such as the F-distribution is a division of two chi-square distributions, the normal distribution is a sum of multiple uniform distributions, and so forth. To illustrate how this works, consider the cumulative distribution function (CDF) of a joint probability distribution between the two random variables X and Y:

$$F_{X+Y}(u) = \iint_{x+y \leq u} f(x,y)dxdy = \int_{-\infty}^{\infty} \left(\int_{y=-\infty}^{u-x} f(x,y)\,dy \right) dx$$

Differentiating the CDF equation above yields the PDF:

$$f_{X+Y}(u) = \int_{-\infty}^{\infty} f(x, u-x)dx$$

Example 1: The convolution of the simple sum of two identical and independent uniform distributions approaches the triangular distribution.

As a simple example, if we take the sum of two *i.i.d.* uniform distributions with a minimum of 0 and maximum of 1, we have:

$$f_{X+Y}(u) = \int_{-\infty}^{\infty} f(x)f(u-x)dx$$

where for a uniform $[0, 1]$ distribution, $f(x) = 1$ when $0 \leq x \leq 1$, we have:

$$f_{X+Y}(u) = \int_0^1 f(u-x)dx = \int_{u-1}^u f(t)dt = \begin{cases} u & u \leq 1 \\ 2-u & 1 < u \leq 2 \end{cases}$$

which approaches a simple triangular distribution.

Figure 7.1 shows an empirical approach where two uniform $[0, 1]$ distributions are simulated for 20,000 trials and their sums added. The computed empirical sums are then extracted and the raw data fitted using the Kolmogorov–Smirnov fitting algorithm in Risk Simulator. The triangular distribution appears as the best-fitting distribution with a 74% goodness-of-fit. As seen in the convolution of only two uniform distributions, the result is a simple triangular distribution.

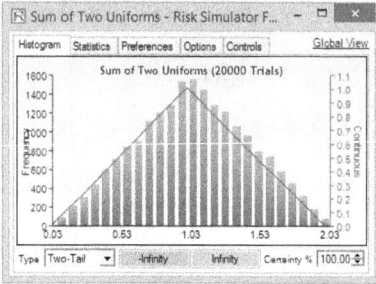

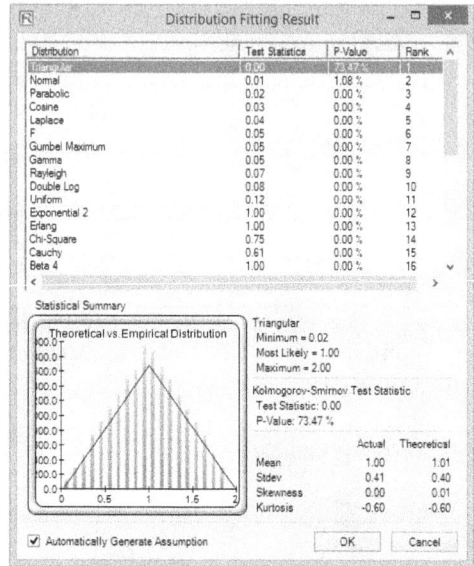

Figure 7.1: Convolution of Two Uniform Distributions via Simulation

Example 2: The convolution simple sum of 12 identical and independent uniform distributions approaches the normal distribution.

If we take the same approach as used in Example 1 and simulate 12 *i.i.d.* uniform [0, 1] distributions and sum them, we would obtain a very close to perfect normal distribution as shown in Figure 7.2, with a goodness-of-fit at 99.3% after running 20,000 simulation trials.

Example 2: Uniform + Uniform + ... + Uniform = Normal

Uniform 1 (0,1):	0.5
Uniform 2 (0,1):	0.5
Uniform 3 (0,1):	0.5
Uniform 4 (0,1):	0.5
Uniform 5 (0,1):	0.5
Uniform 6 (0,1):	0.5
Uniform 7 (0,1):	0.5
Uniform 8 (0,1):	0.5
Uniform 9 (0,1):	0.5
Uniform 10 (0,1):	0.5
Uniform 11 (0,1):	0.5
Uniform 12 (0,1):	0.5
Sum:	6.00

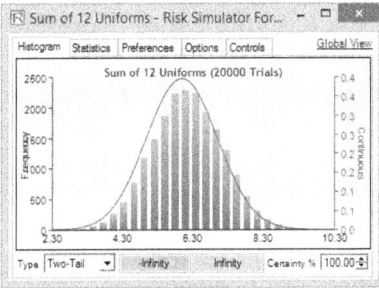

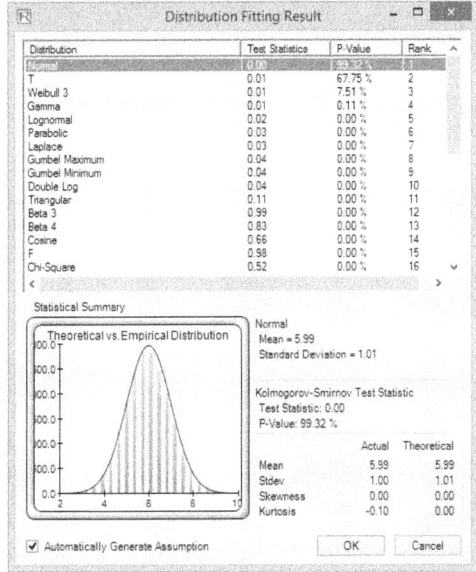

Distribution Fitting Result

Distribution	Test Statistics	P-Value	Rank
Normal	0.00	99.32 %	1
T	0.01	67.75 %	2
Weibull 3	0.01	7.51 %	3
Gamma	0.01	0.11 %	4
Lognormal	0.02	0.00 %	5
Parabolic	0.03	0.00 %	6
Laplace	0.03	0.00 %	7
Gumbel Maximum	0.04	0.00 %	8
Gumbel Minimum	0.04	0.00 %	9
Double Log	0.04	0.00 %	10
Triangular	0.11	0.00 %	11
Beta 3	0.99	0.00 %	12
Beta 4	0.83	0.00 %	13
Cosine	0.66	0.00 %	14
F	0.98	0.00 %	15
Chi-Square	0.52	0.00 %	16

Statistical Summary

Theoretical vs. Empirical Distribution

Normal
Mean = 5.99
Standard Deviation = 1.01

Kolmogorov-Smirnov Test Statistic
Test Statistic: 0.00
P-Value: 99.32 %

	Actual	Theoretical
Mean	5.99	5.99
Stdev	1.00	1.01
Skewness	0.00	0.00
Kurtosis	-0.10	0.00

☑ Automatically Generate Assumption   OK   Cancel

Sum of 12 Uniforms - Risk Simulator For...

Histogram | Statistics | Preferences | Options | Controls   Global View

Sum of 12 Uniforms (20000 Trials)

Type Two-Tail ▼ -Infinity Infinity Certainty % 100.00 ⊕

Figure 7.2: Convolution of 12 Uniform Distributions to Create a Normal

Example 3: The convolution simple sum of multiple identical and independent exponential distributions approaches the gamma (Erlang) distribution.

In this example, we sum two *i.i.d.* exponential distributions and generalize it to multiple distributions. To get started, we use two identical exponential $[\lambda = 2]$ distributions:

$$f_{X+Y}(z) = \int_0^Z f_X(x)f_Y(z-x)dx = \int_0^Z \lambda e^{-\lambda X}\lambda e^{-\lambda(Z-X)}dx = \lambda^2 z e^{-\lambda Z}$$

where $f(x) = \lambda e^{-\lambda X}$ is the PDF for the exponential distribution for all $x \geq 0; \lambda \geq 0$, and the distribution's mean is $\beta = 1/\lambda$.

If we generalize to n random *i.i.d.* exponential distributions and apply mathematical induction:

$$f_{X_1+X_2+...+X_n}(x) = \frac{x^{n-1}e^{-x/\beta}}{(n-1)!\beta^n} = \Gamma[0, n, 1/\lambda]$$

$$f(x) = \frac{x^{\alpha-1}e^{-x/\beta}}{\Gamma(\alpha)\beta^\alpha} \quad \text{with any value of } \alpha > 0 \text{ and } \beta > 0$$

This is, of course, the generalized gamma distribution with α and β for the shape and scale parameters:

$$f_{X_1+X_2+\ldots+X_n}(x) = \Gamma[0, n, 1/\lambda] = \Gamma[0, \alpha, \beta]$$

When the β parameter is a positive integer, the gamma distribution is called the Erlang distribution, used to predict waiting times in queuing systems, where the Erlang distribution is the sum of random variables each having a memoryless exponential distribution. Setting n as the number of these random variables, the mathematical construct of the Erlang distribution is:

$$f(x) = \frac{x^{\alpha-1}e^{-x}}{(\alpha-1)!} \text{ for all } x > 0 \text{ and all positive integers of } \alpha$$

The empirical approach is shown in Figure 7.3, where we have two exponential distributions with $\lambda = 2$ (this means that the mean $\beta = 1/\lambda = 0.5$). The sum of these two distributions, after running 20,000 Monte Carlo simulation trials and extracting and fitting the raw simulated sum data (Figure 7.3), shows a 99.4% goodness-of-fit when fitted to the gamma distribution where the $\alpha = 2$ and $\beta = 0.5$ (rounded), corresponding to $n = 2$ and $\lambda = 2$.

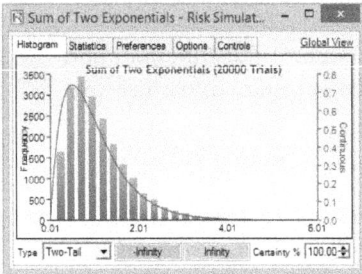

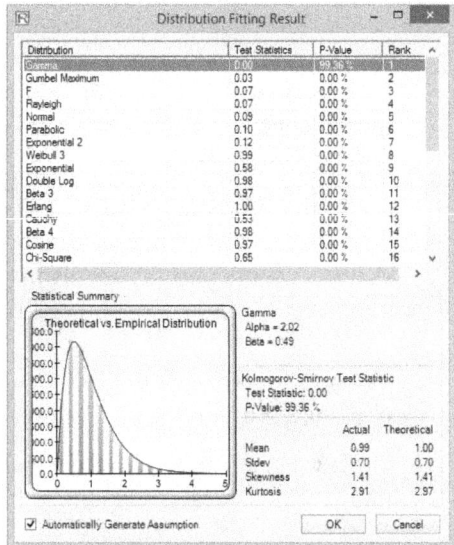

Figure 7.3: Convolution of Exponentials to Create a Gamma Erlang

A copula is a multivariate probability distribution for which the marginal probability distribution of each variable is uniform. Copulas are used to describe the dependence between random variables and are typically used to model distributions that are correlated with one another.

The standard definition of copulas is based on Sklar's Theorem, which states that an m-dimensional copula (or m-copula) is a function C from the unit m-cube $[0, 1]^m$ to the unit interval $[0, 1]$ that satisfies the following conditions:

$$C(1,\ldots,1,a_n,1,\ldots,1) = a_n \text{ for } n \leq m \text{ and all } a_n \text{ in } [0,1]$$

$$C(a_1,\ldots,a_m) = 0 \text{ } if \text{ } a_n = 0 \text{ for any } n \leq m \text{ where } C \text{ is } m - \text{increasing}$$

Consider a continuous m-variate distribution function $F(y_1,\ldots,y_m)$ with univariate marginal distributions $F_1(y_1),\ldots,F_m(y_m)$ and inverse quantile functions $F_1^{-1},\ldots,F_m^{-1}$. Then we have $y_1 = F_1^{-1}(u_1) \sim F_1,\ldots,y_m = F_m^{-1}(u_m) \sim F_m$, where $u_1,\ldots,u_m$ are uniformly distributed variates. Therefore, the transforms of uniform variates are distributed as $F_i (i = 1,\ldots,m)$. This means we have:

$$F(y_1,\ldots,y_m) = F[F_1^{-1}(u_1),\ldots,F_m^{-1}(u_m)]$$
$$F(y_1,\ldots,y_m) = P[U_1 \leq u_1,\ldots,U_m \leq u_m]$$
$$F(y_1,\ldots,y_m) = C[u_1,\ldots,u_m]$$

where C is the unique copula associated with the distribution function. That is, $y \sim F$, and F is continuous, then $F_1(y_1),\ldots,F_m(y_m) \sim C$ and if $U \sim C$, then we have $F_1^{-1}(u_1),\ldots,F_m^{-1}(u_m) \sim F$. Mathematical algorithms using Iman–Conover and Cholesky decomposition matrices are used to compute the joint marginal distributions. Copulas are parametrically specified joint distributions generated from given marginals. Therefore, properties of copulas are analogous to properties of joint distributions.

PROS AND CONS OF CONVOLUTION AND COPULA

Convolution theory is applicable and elegant for theoretical constructs of probability distributions. With basic addition, multiplication, and division of known *i.i.d.* distributions, we can determine its theoretical outputs. The issue with convolution theory is that there are no correlations (independently distributed) between the random variables and their distributions, and the individual distributions have to be exactly the same (identically distributed) and commonly known.

Therefore, if one modifies the distributions, uses exotic distributions, mixes and matches different non–*i.i.d.* distributions, adds correlations, creates large Excel models (beyond the simple addition, multiplication, or division as shown above, such as when there are exotic financial models and computations), and uses truncation, empirical nonparametric distributions, historical simulation, and other combinations of such issues, convolution will not work and cannot predict the outcomes. In addition, both convolution and copula theorems can only be used to compute correlations of joint distributions but would be limited to only a few distributions before the mathematics become intractable due to the large matrix inversions, multiple integrals, and differential equations that need to be solved. Therefore, analysts are restricted to using Monte Carlo risk simulations.

APPLIED EXAMPLE: CONVOLUTION OF MULTIPLICATION OF FREQUENCY AND SEVERITY DISTRIBUTIONS IN OPERATIONAL RISK CAPITAL MODEL IN BASEL III

In October 2014, the Basel Committee on Banking Supervision released a Basel Consultative Document entitled, "Operational Risk: Revisions to the Simpler Approaches," and in it describes the concepts of operational risk as the sum product of frequency and severity of risk events within a one-year time frame and defines the Operational Capital at Risk (OPCAR) as the tail-end 99.9% Value at Risk (VaR). The Basel Consultative Document describes a Single Loss Approximation (SLA) model defined as $F_S^{-1}(p) = F_X^{-1}\left[1 - \frac{1-p}{\lambda}\right] + (\lambda - 1)E[X]$, where the inverse of the compound distribution F_S^{-1} is the summation of the unexpected losses $UL = F_X^{-1}\left[1 - \frac{1-p}{\lambda}\right]$ and expected losses $EL = (\lambda - 1)E[X]$; λ is the Poisson distribution's input parameter (average frequency per period; in this case, 12 months); and X represents one of several types of continuous probability distributions representing the severity of the losses (e.g., Pareto, log logistic, etc.). The Document further states that this is an approximation model limited to subexponential-type distributions only and is fairly difficult to compute. The X distribution's cumulative distribution function (CDF) will need to be inverted using Fourier transform methods, and the results are only approximations based on a limited set of inputs and their requisite constraints. Also, as discussed below, the SLA model proposed in the Basel Consultative Document significantly underestimates OPCAR.

This current chapter provides a new and alternative convolution methodology to compute OPCAR that is applicable across a large variety of continuous probability distributions for risk severity and includes a comparison of their results with Monte Carlo risk simulation methods. As will be shown, both the new algorithm using numerical methods to model OPCAR and the Monte Carlo risk simulation approach tend to the same results, and seeing that simulation can be readily and easily applied in the CMOL software and Risk Simulator software, we recommend using simulation methodologies for the sake of simplicity. While the Basel Committee has, throughout its Basel II-III requirements and recommendations, sought after simplicity so as not to burden banks with added complexity, it still requires sufficient rigor and substantiated theory. Monte Carlo risk simulation methods pass the test on both fronts and are, hence, the recommended path when modeling OPCAR.

Problem with Basel OPCAR

We submit that the SLA estimation model proposed in the Basel Consultative Document is insufficient and significantly underestimates an actual OPCAR value. A cursory examination shows that with various λ values, such as $\lambda = 1$, $\lambda = 10$, $\lambda = 100$, $\lambda = 1000$, the $UL = F_X^{-1}\left[1 - \frac{1-p}{\lambda}\right]$ will yield $\left[1 - \frac{1-p}{\lambda}\right]$ probability values (η) of 0.999, 0.9999, 0.99999, and 0.999999. $UL = F_X^{-1}[\eta]$ for any severity distribution X will only yield the severity distribution's values, and not the total unexpected losses. For instance, suppose the severity distribution (X) of a single risk event on average ranges from \$1M (minimum) to \$2M (maximum), and, for simplicity, assume it is a uniformly distributed severity of losses. Further suppose that the average frequency of events is 1,000 times per year. Based on back of the envelop calculation, one could then conclude that the absolute highest operational risk capital losses will never exceed \$2B per year (this assumes the absolute worst case scenario of \$2M loss per event multiplied by 1,000 events in that entire year). Nonetheless, using the inverse of the X distribution at $\eta = 0.999999$ will yield a value close to $2M only, and adding that to the adjusted expected value of expected losses or EL (let's just assume somewhere close to $1.5B based on the uniform distribution) is still a far cry from the upper end of $2B.

Figure 7.4 shows a more detailed calculation that proves the Basel Consultative Document's SLA approximation method significantly understates the true distributional operational value at risk amount. In the figure, we test four examples of a Poisson–Weibull convolution. The Poisson distribution with lambda risk event frequency $\lambda = 10$, $\lambda = 25$, $\lambda = 50$, and $\lambda = 100$ are tested, together with a Weibull risk severity distribution of $\alpha = 1.5$ and $\beta = 2.5$. These values are shown as highlighted cells in the figure. Using the Basel OPCAR model, we compute the UL and EL. In the unexpected losses or UL computation, we use $UL = F_X^{-1}\left[1 - \frac{1-p}{\lambda}\right] = F_X^{-1}[\eta]$. The column labeled PROB is η. The ICDF X column denotes the $UL = F_X^{-1}[\eta]$. By applying the inverse of the Weibull CDF on the probability, we obtain the UL values. Next, the EL calculations are simply $EL = (\lambda - 1)E[X]$ with $E[X]$ being the expected value of the Weibull distribution X, where $E[X] = \beta\Gamma[1 + 1/\alpha]$. The OPCAR is simply $UL + EL$. The four OPCAR results obtained are 31.30, 65.87, 122.82, and 236.18.

We then tested the results using Monte Carlo risk simulation using the Risk Simulator software (www.realoptionsvaluation.com) by setting four Poisson distributions with their respective λ values and a single Weibull distribution with $\alpha = 1.5$ and $\beta = 2.5$. Then, the Weibull distribution is multiplied by each of the Poisson distributions to obtain the four Total Loss Distributions. The simulation was run for 100,000 trials and the results are shown in Figure 7.4 as forecast charts at the bottom. The left tail $\leq 99.9\%$ quantile values were obtained and can be seen in the charts (116.38, 258.00, 476.31, and 935.25). These are significantly higher than the four OPCAR results.

Next, we ran a third approach using the newly revised convolution algorithm we propose in this chapter. The convolution model shows the same values as the Monte Carlo risk simulation results: 116.38, 258.00, 476.31, and 935.25, when rounded to two decimals. The inverse of the convolution function computes the corresponding CDF percentiles and they are all 99.9% (rounded to one decimal; see the Convolution and Percentile columns in Figure 7.4). Using the same inverse of the convolution function and applied to the Basel Consultative Document's SLA model results, we found that the four SLA results were at the following OPCAR percentiles: 75.75%, 66.94%, 62.78%, and 60.38%, again significantly different than the requisite 99.9% Value at Risk level for operational risk capital required by the Basel Committee.

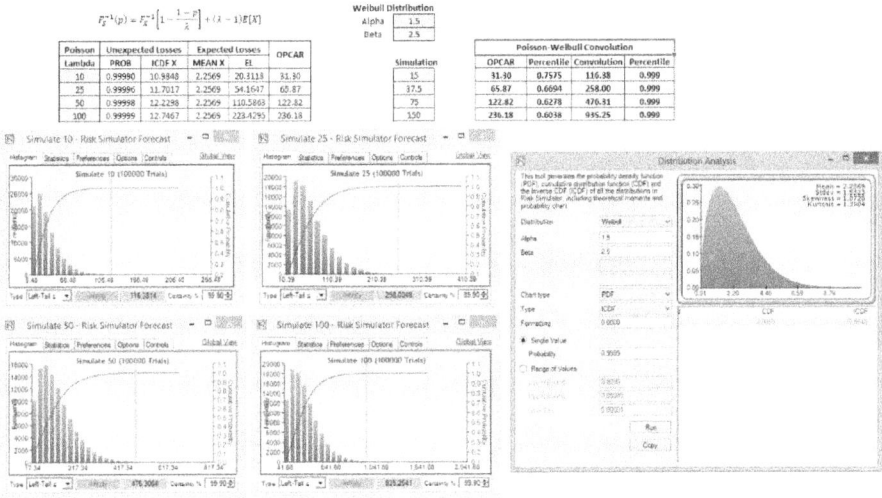

Figure 7.4: Comparing Basel OPCAR, Monte Carlo Risk Simulation, and the Convolution Algorithm

Therefore, due to this significant understatement of operational capital at risk, the remainder of this chapter focuses on explaining the theoretical details of the newly revised convolution model we developed that provides exact OPCAR results under certain conditions. We then compare the results using Monte Carlo risk simulation methods using Risk Simulator software as well as the Credit, Market, Operational, and Liquidity (CMOL) Risk software (source: www.realoptionsvaluation.com). Finally, the caveats and limitations of this new approach as well as conclusions and recommendations are presented.

Theory

Let X, Y, and Z be real-valued random variables whereby X and Y are independently distributed with no correlations. Further, we define F_X, F_Y, and F_Z as their corresponding CDFs, and f_X, f_Y, f_Z are their corresponding PDFs. Next, we assume that X is a random variable denoting the frequency of a certain type of operational risk occurring and is further assumed to have a discrete Poisson distribution. Y is a random variable denoting the severity of the risk (e.g., monetary value or some other economic value) and can be distributed from among a group of continuous distributions (e.g., Fréchet, gamma, log logistic, lognormal, Pareto, Weibull, etc.). Therefore, *Frequency* $\times$ *Severity* equals the *Total Risk Losses*, which we define as Z, where $Z = X \times Y$.

Then the Total Loss formula, which is also sometimes known as the Single Loss Approximation (SLA) model, yields:

$$F_Z(t) = P(Z < t) = \sum_k P(XY < t \mid X = k) \times P(X = k)$$

$$F_Z(t) = P(Z < t) = \sum_k P(kY < t) \times P(X = k)$$

where the term with $X = 0$ is treated separately:

$$F_Z(t) = P(0 < t|X = 0) \times P(X = 0) + \sum_{k \neq 0} P(Y < t/k) \times P(X = k)$$

$$F_Z(t) = \sum_{k \neq 0} f_X(k) F_Y(t/k) + P(X = 0) \qquad \text{(Equation 1)}$$

The next step is the selection of the number of summands in Equation 1. As previously assumed, $f_X(k) = P(X = k)$ is a Poisson distribution where $P(X = k) = \frac{\lambda^k e^{-\lambda}}{k!}$ and the rate of convergence in the series depends solely on the rate of convergence to 0 of $\frac{\lambda^k}{k!}$ and does not depend on t, whereas the second multiplier $P(Y < t/k) \leq 1$! Therefore, for all values of t and an arbitrary $\delta > 0$, there is value of n such that:

$$\sum_{k>n} \frac{\lambda^k e^{-\lambda}}{k!} F_Y(t/k) < \delta \qquad \text{(Equation 2)}$$

In our case, δ can be set, for example, to $1/1000$. Thus, instead of solving the quantile equation for t_p with an infinite series, on the left-hand side of the equation we have:

$$F_Z(t) = P(Z < t) = \sum_k P\left(Y < \frac{t}{k}\right) \frac{\lambda^k e^{-\lambda}}{k!} = p \qquad \text{(Equation 3)}$$

We can then solve the equation:

$$F_Z(t, n) = \sum_{k \le n} \frac{\lambda^k e^{-\lambda}}{k!} F_Y(t/k) = p \qquad \text{(Equation 4)}$$

with only n summands.

For example, if we choose $p = 0.95$, $\delta = 1/1000$, and n such that Equation 2 takes place, then the solution $t_p(n)$ of Equation 4 is such that:

$$\left| F_Z\big(t_p(n)\big) - F_Z\big(t_p(n), n\big) \right| < 1/1000 \qquad \text{(Equation 5)}$$

In other words, a quantile found from Equation 4 is almost the true value, with a resulting error precision in probability of less than 0.1%.

The only outstanding issue that remains is to find an estimate for n given any level of δ. We have:

$$\sum_{k>n} \frac{\lambda^k e^{-\lambda}}{k!} F_Y(t/k) < e^{-\lambda} \sum_{k>n} \frac{\lambda^k}{k!} \qquad \text{(Equation 6)}$$

The exponential series $R_n(\lambda) = \sum_{k>n} \frac{\lambda^k}{k!}$ in Equation 6 is bounded by $\frac{\lambda^{n+1} e^{\lambda}}{(n+1)!}$ by applying the Taylor's Expansion Theorem, with the remainder of the function left for higher exponential function expansions. By substituting the upper bound for $R_n(\lambda)$ in Equation 6, we have:

$$\sum_{k>n} \frac{\lambda^k e^{-\lambda}}{k!} F_Y(t/k) < \frac{\lambda^{n+1}}{(n+1)!} \qquad \text{(Equation 7)}$$

Now we need to find the lower bound in n for the solution of the inequality:

$$\frac{\lambda^{n+1}}{(n+1)!} < \delta \qquad \text{(Equation 8)}$$

Consider the following two cases:

1. If $\lambda \le 1$, then $\frac{\lambda^{n+1}}{(n+1)!} \le \frac{1}{(n+1)!} \le (n+1)^{-(n+1)} e^n$. Consequently, we can solve the inequality $(n+1)^{-(n+1)} e^n < \delta$. Since n^n grows quickly, we can simply take $n > -\ln \delta$. For example, for $\delta = 1/1000$, it is sufficient to set $n = 7$ to satisfy Equation 8.

2. If $\lambda > 1$, then, in this case, using the same bounds for the factorial, we can choose n such that:

$$(n+1)(\ln(n+1) - \ln\lambda - 1) > -\ln\delta - 1$$

$$\text{(Equation 9)}$$

To make the second multiplier greater than 1, we will need to choose $n > e^{2+\ln\lambda} - 1$.

Approximation to the solution of the equation $F_Z(t) = p$ for a quantile value

From the previous considerations we found that instead of solving $F_Z(t) = p$ for t, we can solve $F_Z(t, n) = \sum_{k \le n} \frac{\lambda^k e^{-\lambda}}{k!} F_Y(t/k) = p$ with n set at the level indicated above. The value for t_p resulting from such a substitution will satisfy the inequality $|F_Z(t_p(n)) - F_Z(t_p(n), n)| < \delta$.

Solution of the equation $F_Z(t, n) = p$ given n and δ

By moving t to the left one unit at a time, we can find the first occurrence of the event $t = a$ such that $F_Z(a, n) \le p$. Similarly, moving t to the right we can find b such that $F_Z(b, n) \ge p$. Now we can use a simple Bisection Method or other search algorithms to find the optimal solution to $F_Z(t, n) = p$.

EMPIRICAL RESULTS: CONVOLUTION VERSUS MONTE CARLO RISK SIMULATION FOR OPCAR

Based on the explanations and algorithms outlined above, the convolution approximation models are run and results compared with Monte Carlo risk simulation results. These comparisons will serve as empirical evidence of the applicability of both approaches.

Figure 7.5 shows the 10 most commonly used severity distributions, namely, exponential, Fréchet, gamma, logistic, log logistic, lognormal (arithmetic and logarithmic inputs), Gumbel, Pareto, and Weibull. The frequency of risk occurrences is set as Poisson, with lambda (λ) or average frequency rate per period as its input. The input parameters for the 10 severity distributions are typically alpha (α) and beta (β), except for the exponential distribution that uses a rate parameter, rho (ρ), and lognormal distribution that requires the mean (μ) and standard deviation (σ) as inputs. For the first empirical test, we set $\lambda = 10$, $\alpha = 1.5$, $\beta = 2.5$, $\rho = 0.01$, $\mu = 1.8$, and $\sigma = 0.5$ for the Poisson frequency and 10 severity distributions. The Convolution Model row in Figure 7.5 was computed using the algorithms outlined above, and a set of Monte Carlo risk simulation assumptions were set with the same input parameters and simulated 100,000 trials with a prespecified seed value. The results from the simulation were pasted back into the model under the Simulated Results row and the Convolution Model was calculated based on these simulated outputs. Figure 7.5 shows 5 sets of simulation percentiles: 99.9%, 99.0%,

95.0%, 90.0%, and 50.0%. As can be seen, all of the simulation results and the convolution results on average agree to approximately within ±0.2%.

Figure 7.6 shows another empirical test whereby we select one specific distribution; in the illustration, we used the Poisson–Weibull compound function. The alpha and beta parameters in Weibull were changed, in concert with the Poisson's lambda input. The first four columns show alpha and beta being held steady while changing the lambda parameter, whereas the last six columns show the same lambda with different alpha and beta input values (increasing alpha with beta constant and increasing beta with alpha constant). When the simulation results and the convolution results were compared, on average, they agree to approximately within ±0.2%.

Figure 7.7 shows the Credit, Market, Operational, and Liquidity (CMOL) risk software's operational risk module and how the simulation results agree with the convolution model. The CMOL software uses the algorithms as described above. Its settings are 100,000 Simulation Trials with a Seed Value of 1 with an OPCAR set to 99.90%.

Figures 7.8–7.11 show additional empirical tests where all 10 severity distributions were perturbed, convoluted, and compared with the simulation results. The results agree on average around ±0.3%.

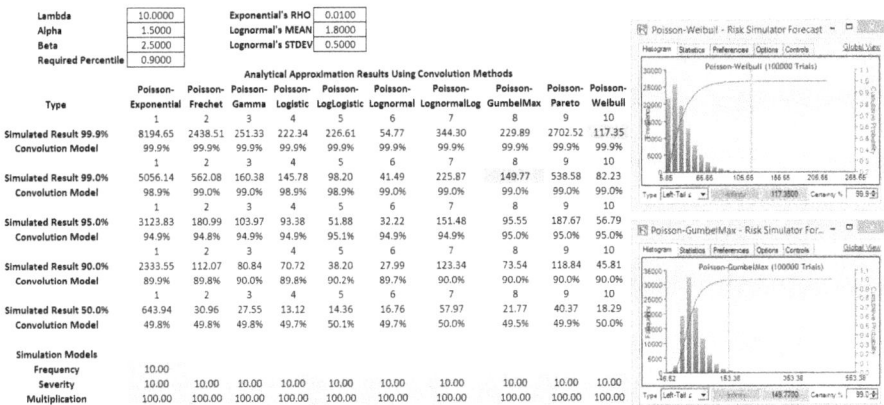

Lambda	10.0000		Exponential's RHO	0.0100
Alpha	1.5000		Lognormal's MEAN	1.8000
Beta	2.5000		Lognormal's STDEV	0.5000
Required Percentile	0.9000			

	Analytical Approximation Results Using Convolution Methods									
Type	Poisson-Exponential	Poisson-Frechet	Poisson-Gamma	Poisson-Logistic	Poisson-LogLogistic	Poisson-Lognormal	Poisson-LognormalLog	Poisson-GumbelMax	Poisson-Pareto	Poisson-Weibull
	1	2	3	4	5	6	7	8	9	10
Simulated Result 99.9%	8194.65	2438.51	251.33	222.34	226.61	54.77	344.30	229.89	2702.52	117.35
Convolution Model	99.9%	99.9%	99.9%	99.9%	99.9%	99.9%	99.9%	99.9%	99.9%	99.9%
	1	2	3	4	5	6	7	8	9	10
Simulated Result 99.0%	5056.14	562.08	160.38	145.78	98.20	41.49	225.87	149.77	538.58	82.23
Convolution Model	98.9%	99.0%	99.0%	98.9%	98.9%	99.0%	99.0%	99.0%	99.0%	99.0%
	1	2	3	4	5	6	7	8	9	10
Simulated Result 95.0%	3123.83	180.99	103.97	93.38	51.88	32.22	151.48	95.55	187.67	56.79
Convolution Model	94.9%	94.8%	94.9%	94.9%	95.1%	94.9%	95.0%	95.0%	95.0%	95.0%
	1	2	3	4	5	6	7	8	9	10
Simulated Result 90.0%	2333.55	112.07	80.84	70.72	38.20	27.99	123.34	73.54	118.84	45.81
Convolution Model	89.9%	89.8%	90.0%	89.8%	90.2%	89.7%	90.0%	90.0%	90.0%	90.0%
	1	2	3	4	5	6	7	8	9	10
Simulated Result 50.0%	643.94	30.96	27.55	13.12	14.36	16.76	57.97	21.77	40.37	18.29
Convolution Model	49.8%	49.8%	49.8%	49.7%	50.1%	49.7%	50.0%	49.5%	49.9%	50.0%
Simulation Models										
Frequency	10.00									
Severity	10.00	10.00	10.00	10.00	10.00	10.00	10.00	10.00	10.00	10.00
Multiplication	100.00	100.00	100.00	100.00	100.00	100.00	100.00	100.00	100.00	100.00

Figure 7.5: Comparing Convolution to Simulation Results I

Lambda	10.00	25.00	75.00	100.00	50.00	50.00	50.00	50.00	50.00	50.00
Alpha	1.50	1.50	1.50	1.50	1.50	15.00	45.00	1.50	45.00	1.50
Beta	2.50	2.50	2.50	2.50	2.50	2.50	2.50	15.00	50.00	75.00

Analytical Approximation Results Using Convolution Methods: Weibull Distribution

Type	Poisson-Weibull 1	Poisson-Weibull 2	Poisson-Weibull 3	Poisson-Weibull 4	Poisson-Weibull 5	Poisson-Weibull 6	Poisson-Weibull 7	Poisson-Weibull 8	Poisson-Weibull 9	Poisson-Weibull 10
Simulated Result	117.35	251.52	716.62	943.55	488.72	186.23	183.36	2919.98	3651.15	14629.3
Convolution Model	99.9%	99.9%	99.9%	99.9%	99.9%	99.9%	99.9%	99.9%	99.9%	99.9%
Simulated Result	82.23	185.40	531.75	708.24	362.16	169.24	167.17	2159.08	3339.56	10750.8
Convolution Model	99.0%	98.9%	99.0%	99.0%	99.0%	99.0%	99.0%	99.0%	99.0%	99.0%
Simulated Result	56.79	134.72	393.66	522.88	264.25	154.15	153.77	1589.67	3071.24	7909.56
Convolution Model	95.0%	95.0%	94.9%	94.9%	94.9%	95.0%	95.1%	95.0%	95.0%	94.9%
Simulated Result	45.81	110.63	327.60	437.82	219.00	146.39	146.76	1323.64	2932.39	6579.73
Convolution Model	90.0%	89.8%	89.8%	90.0%	89.8%	90.0%	90.2%	90.1%	90.0%	89.9%
Simulated Result	18.27	47.35	145.21	193.97	96.33	120.06	122.99	578.52	2461.52	2895.14
Convolution Model	50.0%	49.8%	49.9%	49.9%	49.9%	49.8%	50.0%	50.0%	50.2%	50.0%

Simulation Models

Frequency	10.00	25.00	75.00	100.00	50.00	50.00	50.00	50.00	50.00	50.00
Severity	2.26	2.26	2.26	2.26	2.26	2.41	2.47	13.54	49.38	67.71
Multiplication	22.57	56.42	169.26	225.69	112.84	120.71	123.46	677.06	2469.13	3385.29

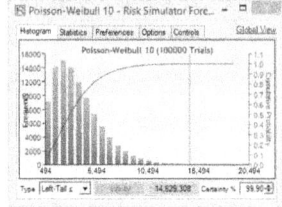

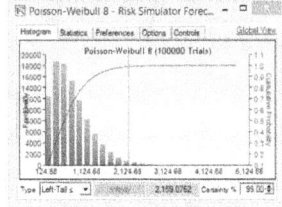

Figure 7.6: Comparing Convolution to Simulation Results II

Lambda	10.00	25.00	75.00
Alpha	1.50	1.50	1.50
Beta	2.50	2.50	2.50

Analytical Approxima

Type	Poisson-Weibull 1	Poisson-Weibull 2	Poisson-Weibull 3
Simulated Result	117.35	251.52	716.62
Convolution Model	99.9%	99.9%	99.9%
Simulated Result	82.23	185.40	531.75
Convolution Model	99.0%	98.9%	99.0%
Type ID	1	2	3
Simulated Result	56.79	134.72	393.66
Convolution Model	95.0%	95.0%	94.9%
Type ID	1	2	3
Simulated Result	45.81	110.63	327.60
Convolution Model	90.0%	89.8%	89.8%
Type ID	1	2	3
Simulated Result	18.27	47.35	145.21
Convolution Model	50.0%	49.8%	49.9%
Simulation Models			
Frequency	10.00	25.00	75.00
Severity	2.26	2.26	2.26
Multiplication	22.57	56.42	169.26

Figure 7.7: Comparing Convolution to Simulation Results III

Frequency: Poisson (λ=10) and Severity: 10 Distributions (α=1.5, β=2.5, ρ=0.01, μ=1.8, σ=0.5)

SIMULATION RESULTS (APPROXIMATE PERCENTILE FROM SIMULATION GIVEN THE LEFT TAIL VALUE)

Exponential	Frechet	Gamma	Logistic	Log Logistic	Lognormal	Lognormal	Gumbel	Pareto	Weibull
99.8%	99.8%	99.8%	99.9%	99.9%	99.8%	99.9%	99.9%	99.8%	99.8%
0.06%	0.08%	0.07%	0.03%	0.04%	0.09%	0.04%	0.03%	0.10%	0.08%
98.9%	99.0%	99.4%	99.0%	98.9%	98.9%	99.0%	98.9%	98.9%	98.9%
0.10%	0.03%	-0.38%	0.00%	0.07%	0.08%	0.05%	0.06%	0.10%	0.10%
94.9%	95.1%	94.7%	95.0%	95.2%	95.0%	94.8%	95.0%	94.9%	95.0%
0.06%	-0.06%	0.35%	0.03%	-0.15%	0.00%	0.21%	0.00%	0.10%	0.01%
90.0%	90.2%	90.1%	90.1%	90.2%	90.0%	90.1%	90.0%	89.9%	90.1%
0.00%	-0.17%	-0.08%	-0.08%	-0.17%	-0.02%	-0.07%	-0.01%	0.10%	-0.12%
50.0%	50.2%	50.1%	50.1%	50.1%	50.1%	50.1%	50.1%	50.0%	50.1%
0.05%	-0.15%	-0.05%	-0.08%	-0.13%	-0.10%	-0.05%	-0.06%	0.01%	-0.11%

Figure 7.8: Empirical Results 1: Small Value Inputs

Frequency: Poisson (λ=50) and Severity: 10 Distributions (α=3, β=5, ρ=0.10, μ=5, σ=1)

SIMULATION RESULTS (APPROXIMATE PERCENTILE FROM SIMULATION GIVEN THE LEFT TAIL VALUE)

Exponential	Frechet	Gamma	Logistic	Log Logistic	Lognormal	Lognormal	Gumbel	Pareto	Weibull
99.9%	99.8%	99.9%	99.8%	99.8%	99.8%	99.8%	99.8%	99.8%	99.8%
0.04%	0.05%	-0.01%	0.06%	0.06%	0.07%	0.06%	0.09%	0.08%	0.09%
98.9%	99.0%	99.0%	99.0%	98.9%	98.9%	99.0%	98.9%	98.9%	98.9%
0.08%	-0.01%	-0.05%	-0.04%	0.08%	0.08%	0.03%	0.06%	0.06%	0.08%
95.0%	95.0%	95.1%	94.9%	95.1%	94.9%	95.0%	94.9%	94.9%	95.1%
-0.02%	-0.02%	-0.05%	0.06%	-0.10%	0.10%	0.03%	0.05%	0.09%	-0.07%
90.2%	90.0%	90.0%	90.0%	90.2%	90.0%	89.9%	90.0%	89.8%	90.1%
-0.15%	-0.03%	0.00%	0.04%	-0.20%	0.00%	0.07%	0.03%	0.16%	-0.05%
49.8%	50.0%	50.0%	50.1%	49.4%	50.0%	50.1%	50.0%	50.0%	50.1%
0.18%	0.00%	0.00%	-0.10%	0.65%	0.00%	-0.10%	0.00%	0.00%	-0.10%

Figure 7.9: Empirical Results 2: Average Value Inputs

Frequency: Poisson (λ=100) and Severity: 10 Distributions (α=25, β=35, ρ=0.025, μ=2.5, σ=0.9)

SIMULATION RESULTS (APPROXIMATE PERCENTILE FROM SIMULATION GIVEN THE LEFT TAIL VALUE)

Exponential	Frechet	Gamma	Logistic	Log Logistic	Lognormal	Lognormal	Gumbel	Pareto	Weibull
99.9%	99.9%	99.8%	99.9%	99.8%	99.8%	99.8%	99.8%	99.9%	99.8%
-0.05%	0.04%	0.06%	0.04%	0.07%	0.07%	0.05%	0.07%	0.03%	0.08%
99.5%	99.0%	99.0%	99.0%	99.0%	99.0%	98.9%	98.9%	98.9%	99.0%
-0.54%	0.03%	0.01%	-0.02%	-0.02%	0.05%	0.10%	0.11%	0.06%	0.01%
97.2%	95.0%	95.2%	95.0%	95.1%	95.0%	95.0%	94.9%	94.9%	95.0%
-2.20%	0.00%	-0.17%	0.00%	-0.10%	0.05%	0.00%	0.15%	0.13%	0.00%
93.7%	90.0%	90.0%	90.0%	90.0%	90.1%	89.9%	90.0%	90.0%	90.3%
-3.70%	0.00%	0.05%	0.00%	0.00%	-0.05%	0.15%	0.00%	0.00%	-0.25%
56.2%	50.0%	50.1%	50.0%	50.0%	50.0%	50.0%	50.1%	50.0%	50.0%
-6.21%	0.00%	-0.05%	-0.01%	-0.01%	0.00%	-0.01%	-0.06%	0.05%	0.00%

Figure 7.10: Empirical Results 3: Medium Value Inputs

Frequency: Poisson (λ=15) and Severity: 10 Distributions (α=80, β=25, ρ=5, μ=25, σ=3)

SIMULATION RESULTS (APPROXIMATE PERCENTILE FROM SIMULATION GIVEN THE LEFT TAIL VALUE)

Exponential	Frechet	Gamma	Logistic	Log Logistic	Lognormal	Lognormal	Gumbel	Pareto	Weibull
99.9%	99.8%	99.9%	99.9%	99.9%	99.8%	99.8%	99.8%	99.9%	99.8%
0.05%	0.06%	0.04%	0.05%	0.03%	0.12%	0.12%	0.08%	0.05%	0.06%
98.9%	98.9%	99.0%	99.0%	99.0%	99.0%	99.0%	98.9%	99.1%	99.0%
0.07%	0.06%	-0.02%	0.03%	0.04%	0.01%	0.01%	0.08%	-0.07%	0.04%
95.0%	95.0%	95.0%	95.1%	95.0%	95.0%	95.0%	95.0%	95.0%	95.0%
0.04%	0.00%	0.01%	-0.06%	0.00%	0.02%	0.02%	0.02%	0.00%	0.05%
90.0%	90.0%	90.2%	90.0%	90.2%	90.0%	90.0%	89.9%	90.0%	90.1%
0.00%	0.00%	-0.16%	0.01%	-0.17%	0.01%	0.01%	0.09%	0.00%	-0.10%
49.9%	50.1%	50.1%	50.0%	49.9%	50.0%	50.0%	50.1%	50.0%	50.0%
0.08%	-0.05%	-0.05%	0.05%	0.10%	0.00%	0.00%	-0.10%	0.00%	0.00%

Figure 7.11: Empirical Results 4: High Value Inputs

HIGH LAMBDA AND LOW LAMBDA LIMITATIONS

As seen in Equation 4, we have the $F_Z(t, n) = \sum_{k \le n} \frac{\lambda^k e^{-\lambda}}{k!} F_Y(t/k) = p$ convolution model. The results are accurate to as many decimal-point precision as desired as long as n is sufficiently large, but this would mean that the convolution model is potentially mathematically intractable. When λ and k are high (the value k depends on the Poisson rate λ), such as $\lambda = 10,000$, the summand cannot be easily computed. For instance, Microsoft Excel 2016 can only compute up to a factorial of 170! where 171! and above returns the #NUM! error. Banks whose operational risks have large λ rate values (extremely high frequency of risk events when all risk types are lumped together into a comprehensive frequency count) have several options: Create a breakdown of the various risk types (broken down by risk categories, by department, by division, etc.) such that the λ is more manageable; use a continuous distribution approximation as shown below; or use Monte Carlo risk simulation techniques, where large λ values will not pose a problem whatsoever.

Poisson distributions with large λ values approach the normal distribution, and we can use this fact to generate an approximation model for the convolution method. The actual deviation between Poisson and normal approximation can be estimated by the Berry–Esseen inequality. For a more accurate and order of magnitude tighter estimation we can use the Wilson–Hilferty approximation instead. For the large lambda situation, we can compute the CDF of the compound of two continuous distributions whose PDFs are defined as $f(x)$ defined on the positive interval of (a, b) for the random variable X, and $g(y)$ defined on the positive interval of (c, d), for the random variable Y. In other words, we have $0 < a < b < \infty$ and $0 < c < d < \infty$. The joint distribution $Z = XY$ has the following characteristics:

$$f(v) = \int_i^j f(x)g(v/x)\frac{1}{x}dx$$

$$F(v) = \int_m^n f(v) = \int\limits_{m\,i}^{n\,j} f(x)g(v/x)\frac{1}{x}dx$$

The integration can be applied analytically using numerical integration methods but the results will critically depend on the integration range of x and v. The values of a, b, c, and d can be computed by taking the inverse CDF of the distributions at 0.01% and 99.99% respectively (e.g., in the normal distribution, this allows us to obtain real values instead of relying on the theoretical tails of $-\infty$ and $+\infty$).

The following table summarizes the integration ranges:

When $AD < BC$:	When $AD = BC$:	When $AD > BC$:
$j = v/c$ if $ac < v$ $< ad$	$j = v/c$ if $ac < v$ $< ad$	$j = v/c$ if $ac < v$ $< bc$
$j = v/c$ if $ad < v$ $< bc$	$j = b$ if $ad < v$ $< bd$	$j = b$ if $bc < v < ad$
$j = b$ if $bc < v < bd$	$i = a$ if $ac < v < ad$	$j = b$ if $ad < v$ $< bd$
$i = a$ if $ac < v < ad$	$i = v/d$ if $ad < v$ $< bd$	$i = a$ if $ac < v < bc$
$i = v/d$ if $ad < v$ $< bc$		$i = a$ if $bc < v < ad$
$i = v/d$ if $bc < v$ $< bd$		$i = v/d$ if $ad < v$ $< bd$

To obtain the values of m and n, we can first run a Monte Carlo Risk Simulation of the two independent distributions, then multiply them to obtain the joint distribution, and from this joint distribution, we obtain the left tail 0.01% value, and set this as m. The value of n is the left tail VaR% (e.g., 99.95%) value. The second integral when run based on this range, will return the CDF percentile of the OPCAR VaR. Alternatively, as previously described, the Bisection Method can be used to obtain the lowest value of m by performing iterative searches such that the CDF returns valid results at 0.01%, and then a second search is performed to identify the upper range or n, where the resulting n makes the integral equal to the user specified VaR%, that is, the OPCAR value.

Finally, for low lambda values, the algorithm still runs but will be a lot less accurate. Recall in Equation 2 that $\sum_{k>n} \frac{\lambda^k e^{-\lambda}}{k!} F_Y(t/k) < \delta$ where δ signifies the level of error precision (the lower the value, the higher the precision and accuracy of the results). The problem is, with low λ values, both k and n, which depend on λ, will also be low. This means that in the summand there would be an insufficient number of integer intervals, making the summation function less accurate. For best results, λ should be between 5 and 100.

CAVEATS, CONCLUSIONS, AND RECOMMENDATIONS

Based on the theory, application, and empirical evidence above, one can conclude that the convolution of *Frequency* × *Severity* independent stochastic random probability distributions can be modeled using the algorithms outlined above as well as using Monte Carlo simulation methods. On average, the results from these two methods tend to converge with some slight percentage variation due to randomness in the simulation process and the precision depending on the number of intervals in the summand or numerical integration techniques employed. However, as noted, the algorithms described above are only applicable when the lambda parameter $5 \leq \lambda \leq 100$, else the approximation using numerical integration approach is required. In contrast, Monte Carlo risk simulation methods are applicable in any realistic lambda situation (in simulation, a high lambda condition can be treated by using a normal distribution). As both the numerical method and simulation approach tend to the same results, and seeing that simulation can be readily and easily applied in CMOL and using Risk Simulator, we recommend using simulation methodologies for the sake of simplicity. The Basel Committee has, throughout its Basel II-III requirements and recommendations, sought for simplicity so as not to burden the banks with added complexity, and yet it still requires sufficient rigor and substantiated theory. Therefore, Monte Carlo risk simulation methods are the recommended path when it comes to modeling OPCAR.

Partial Area Standard Normal (Z)

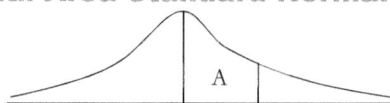

Z	0.00	0.01	0.02	0.03	0.04	0.05	0.06	0.07	0.08	0.09
0.0	0.0000	0.0040	0.0080	0.0120	0.0160	0.0199	0.0239	0.0279	0.0319	0.0359
0.1	0.0398	0.0438	0.0478	0.0517	0.0557	0.0596	0.0636	0.0675	0.0714	0.0753
0.2	0.0793	0.0832	0.0871	0.0910	0.0948	0.0987	0.1026	0.1064	0.1103	0.1141
0.3	0.1179	0.1217	0.1255	0.1293	0.1331	0.1368	0.1406	0.1443	0.1480	0.1517
0.4	0.1554	0.1591	0.1628	0.1664	0.1700	0.1736	0.1772	0.1808	0.1844	0.1879
0.5	0.1915	0.1950	0.1985	0.2019	0.2054	0.2088	0.2123	0.2157	0.2190	0.2224
0.6	0.2257	0.2291	0.2324	0.2357	0.2389	0.2422	0.2454	0.2486	0.2517	0.2549
0.7	0.2580	0.2611	0.2642	0.2673	0.2704	0.2734	0.2764	0.2794	0.2823	0.2852
0.8	0.2881	0.2910	0.2939	0.2967	0.2995	0.3023	0.3051	0.3078	0.3106	0.3133
0.9	0.3159	0.3186	0.3212	0.3238	0.3264	0.3289	0.3315	0.3340	0.3365	0.3389
1.0	0.3413	0.3438	0.3461	0.3485	0.3508	0.3531	0.3554	0.3577	0.3599	0.3621
1.1	0.3643	0.3665	0.3686	0.3708	0.3729	0.3749	0.3770	0.3790	0.3810	0.3830
1.2	0.3849	0.3869	0.3888	0.3907	0.3925	0.3944	0.3962	0.3980	0.3997	0.4015
1.3	0.4032	0.4049	0.4066	0.4082	0.4099	0.4115	0.4131	0.4147	0.4162	0.4177
1.4	0.4192	0.4207	0.4222	0.4236	0.4251	0.4265	0.4279	0.4292	0.4306	0.4319
1.5	0.4332	0.4345	0.4357	0.4370	0.4382	0.4394	0.4406	0.4418	0.4429	0.4441
1.6	0.4452	0.4463	0.4474	0.4484	0.4495	0.4505	0.4515	0.4525	0.4535	0.4545
1.7	0.4554	0.4564	0.4573	0.4582	0.4591	0.4599	0.4608	0.4616	0.4625	0.4633
1.8	0.4641	0.4649	0.4656	0.4664	0.4671	0.4678	0.4686	0.4693	0.4699	0.4706
1.9	0.4713	0.4719	0.4726	0.4732	0.4738	0.4744	0.4750	0.4756	0.4761	0.4767
2.0	0.4772	0.4778	0.4783	0.4788	0.4793	0.4798	0.4803	0.4808	0.4812	0.4817
2.1	0.4821	0.4826	0.4830	0.4834	0.4838	0.4842	0.4846	0.4850	0.4854	0.4857
2.2	0.4861	0.4864	0.4868	0.4871	0.4875	0.4878	0.4881	0.4884	0.4887	0.4890
2.3	0.4893	0.4896	0.4898	0.4901	0.4904	0.4906	0.4909	0.4911	0.4913	0.4916
2.4	0.4918	0.4920	0.4922	0.4925	0.4927	0.4929	0.4931	0.4932	0.4934	0.4936
2.5	0.4938	0.4940	0.4941	0.4943	0.4945	0.4946	0.4948	0.4949	0.4951	0.4952
2.6	0.4953	0.4955	0.4956	0.4957	0.4959	0.4960	0.4961	0.4962	0.4963	0.4964
2.7	0.4965	0.4966	0.4967	0.4968	0.4969	0.4970	0.4971	0.4972	0.4973	0.4974
2.8	0.4974	0.4975	0.4976	0.4977	0.4977	0.4978	0.4979	0.4979	0.4980	0.4981
2.9	0.4981	0.4982	0.4982	0.4983	0.4984	0.4984	0.4985	0.4985	0.4986	0.4986
3.0	0.4987	0.4987	0.4987	0.4988	0.4988	0.4989	0.4989	0.4989	0.4990	0.4990

Cumulative Standard Normal (Z)

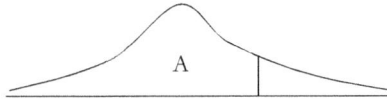

A

Z	0.00	0.01	0.02	0.03	0.04	0.05	0.06	0.07	0.08	0.09
0.0	0.5000	0.5040	0.5080	0.5120	0.5160	0.5199	0.5239	0.5279	0.5319	0.5359
0.1	0.5398	0.5438	0.5478	0.5517	0.5557	0.5596	0.5636	0.5675	0.5714	0.5753
0.2	0.5793	0.5832	0.5871	0.5910	0.5948	0.5987	0.6026	0.6064	0.6103	0.6141
0.3	0.6179	0.6217	0.6255	0.6293	0.6331	0.6368	0.6406	0.6443	0.6480	0.6517
0.4	0.6554	0.6591	0.6628	0.6664	0.6700	0.6736	0.6772	0.6808	0.6844	0.6879
0.5	0.6915	0.6950	0.6985	0.7019	0.7054	0.7088	0.7123	0.7157	0.7190	0.7224
0.6	0.7257	0.7291	0.7324	0.7357	0.7389	0.7422	0.7454	0.7486	0.7517	0.7549
0.7	0.7580	0.7611	0.7642	0.7673	0.7704	0.7734	0.7764	0.7794	0.7823	0.7852
0.8	0.7881	0.7910	0.7939	0.7967	0.7995	0.8023	0.8051	0.8078	0.8106	0.8133
0.9	0.8159	0.8186	0.8212	0.8238	0.8264	0.8289	0.8315	0.8340	0.8365	0.8389
1.0	0.8413	0.8438	0.8461	0.8485	0.8508	0.8531	0.8554	0.8577	0.8599	0.8621
1.1	0.8643	0.8665	0.8686	0.8708	0.8729	0.8749	0.8770	0.8790	0.8810	0.8830
1.2	0.8849	0.8869	0.8888	0.8907	0.8925	0.8944	0.8962	0.8980	0.8997	0.9015
1.3	0.9032	0.9049	0.9066	0.9082	0.9099	0.9115	0.9131	0.9147	0.9162	0.9177
1.4	0.9192	0.9207	0.9222	0.9236	0.9251	0.9265	0.9279	0.9292	0.9306	0.9319
1.5	0.9332	0.9345	0.9357	0.9370	0.9382	0.9394	0.9406	0.9418	0.9429	0.9441
1.6	0.9452	0.9463	0.9474	0.9484	0.9495	0.9505	0.9515	0.9525	0.9535	0.9545
1.7	0.9554	0.9564	0.9573	0.9582	0.9591	0.9599	0.9608	0.9616	0.9625	0.9633
1.8	0.9641	0.9649	0.9656	0.9664	0.9671	0.9678	0.9686	0.9693	0.9699	0.9706
1.9	0.9713	0.9719	0.9726	0.9732	0.9738	0.9744	0.9750	0.9756	0.9761	0.9767
2.0	0.9772	0.9778	0.9783	0.9788	0.9793	0.9798	0.9803	0.9808	0.9812	0.9817
2.1	0.9821	0.9826	0.9830	0.9834	0.9838	0.9842	0.9846	0.9850	0.9854	0.9857
2.2	0.9861	0.9864	0.9868	0.9871	0.9875	0.9878	0.9881	0.9884	0.9887	0.9890
2.3	0.9893	0.9896	0.9898	0.9901	0.9904	0.9906	0.9909	0.9911	0.9913	0.9916
2.4	0.9918	0.9920	0.9922	0.9925	0.9927	0.9929	0.9931	0.9932	0.9934	0.9936
2.5	0.9938	0.9940	0.9941	0.9943	0.9945	0.9946	0.9948	0.9949	0.9951	0.9952
2.6	0.9953	0.9955	0.9956	0.9957	0.9959	0.9960	0.9961	0.9962	0.9963	0.9964
2.7	0.9965	0.9966	0.9967	0.9968	0.9969	0.9970	0.9971	0.9972	0.9973	0.9974
2.8	0.9974	0.9975	0.9976	0.9977	0.9977	0.9978	0.9979	0.9979	0.9980	0.9981
2.9	0.9981	0.9982	0.9982	0.9983	0.9984	0.9984	0.9985	0.9985	0.9986	0.9986
3.0	0.9987	0.9987	0.9987	0.9988	0.9988	0.9989	0.9989	0.9989	0.9990	0.9990

Student's T

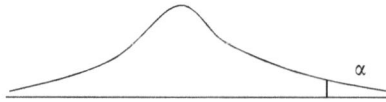

t	0.10	0.05	0.01	0.005		0.10	0.05	0.01	0.005
df 1	3.0777	6.3138	31.8205	63.6567	df 31	1.3095	1.6955	2.4528	2.7440
2	1.8856	2.9200	6.9646	9.9248	32	1.3086	1.6939	2.4487	2.7385
3	1.6377	2.3534	4.5407	5.8409	33	1.3077	1.6924	2.4448	2.7333
4	1.5332	2.1318	3.7469	4.6041	34	1.3070	1.6909	2.4411	2.7284
5	1.4759	2.0150	3.3649	4.0321	35	1.3062	1.6896	2.4377	2.7238
6	1.4398	1.9432	3.1427	3.7074	36	1.3055	1.6883	2.4345	2.7195
7	1.4149	1.8946	2.9980	3.4995	37	1.3049	1.6871	2.4314	2.7154
8	1.3968	1.8595	2.8965	3.3554	38	1.3042	1.6860	2.4286	2.7116
9	1.3830	1.8331	2.8214	3.2498	39	1.3036	1.6849	2.4258	2.7079
10	1.3722	1.8125	2.7638	3.1693	40	1.3031	1.6839	2.4233	2.7045
11	1.3634	1.7959	2.7181	3.1058	41	1.3025	1.6829	2.4208	2.7012
12	1.3562	1.7823	2.6810	3.0545	42	1.3020	1.6820	2.4185	2.6981
13	1.3502	1.7709	2.6503	3.0123	43	1.3016	1.6811	2.4163	2.6951
14	1.3450	1.7613	2.6245	2.9768	44	1.3011	1.6802	2.4141	2.6923
15	1.3406	1.7531	2.6025	2.9467	45	1.3006	1.6794	2.4121	2.6896
16	1.3368	1.7459	2.5835	2.9208	46	1.3002	1.6787	2.4102	2.6870
17	1.3334	1.7396	2.5669	2.8982	47	1.2998	1.6779	2.4083	2.6846
18	1.3304	1.7341	2.5524	2.8784	48	1.2994	1.6772	2.4066	2.6822
19	1.3277	1.7291	2.5395	2.8609	49	1.2991	1.6766	2.4049	2.6800
20	1.3253	1.7247	2.5280	2.8453	50	1.2987	1.6759	2.4033	2.6778
21	1.3232	1.7207	2.5176	2.8314	51	1.2984	1.6753	2.4017	2.6757
22	1.3212	1.7171	2.5083	2.8188	52	1.2980	1.6747	2.4002	2.6737
23	1.3195	1.7139	2.4999	2.8073	53	1.2977	1.6741	2.3988	2.6718
24	1.3178	1.7109	2.4922	2.7969	54	1.2974	1.6736	2.3974	2.6700
25	1.3163	1.7081	2.4851	2.7874	55	1.2971	1.6730	2.3961	2.6682
26	1.3150	1.7056	2.4786	2.7787	56	1.2969	1.6725	2.3948	2.6665
27	1.3137	1.7033	2.4727	2.7707	57	1.2966	1.6720	2.3936	2.6649
28	1.3125	1.7011	2.4671	2.7633	58	1.2963	1.6716	2.3924	2.6633
29	1.3114	1.6991	2.4620	2.7564	59	1.2961	1.6711	2.3912	2.6618
30	1.3104	1.6973	2.4573	2.7500	60	1.2958	1.6706	2.3901	2.6603

SOFTWARE DOWNLOAD & INSTALL

As current versions of the software are continually updated, we highly recommend that you visit the Real Options Valuation, Inc., website and follow the instructions below to install the latest software applications.

- **Step 1**: Visit **www.realoptionsvaluation.com** and click on **Downloads** and **Download Software** (Figure A). You will be prompted to log in. Please first register if you are a first-time user (Figure B) and an automated e-mail will be sent to you within several minutes. (If you do not receive a registration e-mail after you register, then please send a note to support@realoptionsvaluation.com.) While waiting for the automated e-mail, browse this page and see the free getting started videos, case studies, and sample models you can download.

- **Step 2**: Return to this site and LOGIN using the login credentials you received via e-mail. Download and install the latest versions of **Risk Simulator** and **Real Options SLS** on this Web page. The download links, installation instructions, and Hardware ID information are also presented on this page (Figure C).

- **Step 3**: After installing the software, start Excel and you will see a Risk Simulator ribbon. Follow the instructions provided on the Web page to obtain and e-mail support@realoptionsvaluation.com your Hardware ID and mention the code "**MR3E 30 Days**" and you will be sent a free extended 30-day license to use both the Risk Simulator and Real Options SLS software.

www.realoptionsvaluation.com/getting-started-and-modelling-videos/

Testimonials | FAQ | Global Partners | Contact Us

🔤 English ▦ Chinese (Simplified) ▦ Chinese (Traditional) ▐ ▌ French ▬ German ▮ ▮ Italian
🔴 Japanese ✕ Korean 🔷 Portuguese (Brazil) 🔴 Russian ▬ Spanish

Real Options Valuation

0 items $0.00

CQRM CERTIFICATE | TRAINING | CONSULTING | SOFTWARE | BOOKS | DOWNLOADS | PURCHASE |

SOFTWARE DOWNLOADS

GETTING STARTED AND
MODELING VIDEOS

PRODUCT BROCHURES

SAMPLE MODELS

WHITEPAPERS AND CASE STUDIES

DOWNLOAD CENTER

You can also visit our mirror download site if you have problems downloading from this page

Welcome to Real Options Valuation, Inc.'s download center. Here you will be able to download _____ versions of the software you have purchased (license information required to install these full versions), product brochures, case _____ ple training videos to help you get started in using our software, as well as sample Excel models to use with Risk Simulator and Re... _____ ....ftware.

GETTING STARTED AND MODELING VIDEOS

The following are some live-motion and voice narrated videos which are playable on your computer using Windows Media Player or other video players capable of WMV playback. You can simply click on any of these links below to view the streaming videos.

ROV SOFTWARE GETTING STARTED VIDEOS

We also have some more detailed Risk Analysis and Risk Simulator software getting started videos that you can download and watch. These videos total about 2 hours. For even more detailed training, please check out our set of 12 Training DVDs (over 30 hours) or our hands-on Certified in Risk Management seminars (4 days). The following are updated detailed getting started videos on Risk Simulator, featuring all the new tools such as Auto ARIMA, GARCH, JS Curves, Cubic Spline, Maximum Likelihood, Data Diagnostics, Statistical Analysis, Modeling Toolkit, and more...

Figure A: Step 1 – Software download site

DOWNLOAD CENTER

You can also visit our mirror download site if you have problems downloading from this page

Welcome to Real Options Valuation, Inc.'s download center. Here you will be able to download trial versions of our software, full versions of the software you have purchased (license information required to install these full versions), product brochures, case studies and white papers, and sample training videos to help you get started in using our software, as well as sample Excel models to use with Risk Simulator and Real Options Super Lattice Solver software.

YOU ARE REQUIRED TO LOGIN TO VIEW THIS PAGE.

Username

Password

LOG IN   REGISTER

Figure B: Register if you are a first-time visitor

Real Options Valuation

🌐 English ■ Chinese (Simplified) ■ Chinese (Traditional) ■ ■ French ■ German ■ ■ Italian
✳ Japanese ✕ Korean ◆ Portuguese (Brazil) ▬ Russian ▬ Spanish

CQRM CERTIFICATE | TRAINING | CONSULTING | SOFTWARE | BOOKS | DOWNLOADS | PURCHASE |

Items $0.00

FULL & TRIAL VERSION DOWNLOAD:

Download Risk Simulator 2018 – Auto Installer
Download Risk Simulator 2018 – Auto Installer (mirror site)
Download Risk Simulator 2018 – For 32 Bit Excel
Download Risk Simulator 2018 – For 32 Bit Excel (mirror site)
Download Risk Simulator 2018 – For 64 Bit Excel
Download Risk Simulator 2018 – For 64 Bit Excel (mirror site)

Download OLDER version of Risk Simulator 2014 [WIN x64 and Excel x32 edition]
Download OLDER version of Risk Simulator 2014 [WIN x64 and Excel x32 edition] (mirror site)

This is a full version of the software but will expire in 15 days, during which time you can purchase a license to permanently unlock the software. Please first uninstall all previous versions of Risk Simulator before installing this newer version.

To permanently unlock the software, purchase a license and e-mail us your Hardware ID (after installing the software, start Excel, click on Risk Simulator | License, and e-mail admin@realoptionsvaluation.com the 16 to 20 digit Hardware ID located on the bottom left of the splash screen). We will then e-mail you a permanent license file. Save this file to your hard drive, start Excel, click on Risk Simulator, License, Install License and point to the location of this license file, restart Excel and you are now permanently licensed. Installing the license only takes a few seconds.

SYSTEM REQUIREMENTS, FAQ, AND ADDITIONAL RESOURCES:

• Windows 7, 8, and 10 (32 and 64 bits)
• Microsoft Excel 2010, 2013, or 2016
• 2 GB RAM Minimum (4 GB recommended)
• 600 MB Hard Drive
• Administrative Rights to install software
• Microsoft .NET Framework 2.0, 3.0, 3.5 or later
• MAC OS users will require either Virtual Machine or Parallels running Microsoft Excel

Figure C: Download links and hardware ID instructions

INDEX

www.ingramcontent.com/pod-product-compliance
Lightning Source LLC
Chambersburg PA
CBHW060034210326
41520CB00009B/1130